Transitions

The Unheard Stories

jane fae

Published in Great Britain by Trans Media UK on behalf of TransActual

First published September 2024

ISBN: 978-1-7392264-4-2

A Cataloguing in Publication Data record is available from the British Library

Printed in the United Kingdom

Typeset and cover designed by Dorian Rose

Contents

Introduction

Come in. Sit down. Thank you for dropping by.

If you're reading this, I hope that you are genuinely interested in trans people. Listening to trans voices. Hearing a little of what it feels like to 'be trans.' In the UK. Learning. What's it like to transition, against the backdrop of one of the most hostile anti-trans media landscapes in the world, besieged, for the past five years, by a heterodox coalition of politicians, evangelists, and faux feminists, all happy to weaponise the least anti-trans confabulation in their scrabble for votes and influence?

If you want to read a bit more about that, check out international research organisation GATE[1]. Or, alternatively, if you just want to go straight to the stories, skip this bit and maybe come back later.

That said, you may be relieved to learn: this book is not about the politics. Except insofar as political decisions impact the lives of trans people. The beating heart of this book is what it feels like to live through such times. To attempt to remain true to who you know yourself to be, while all around are systems and processes overflowing with 'concerns' and disbelief.

For our own protection, of course. Because heaven forfend that any individual make a decision they might later regret. Though it is a funny, transphobic sort of safeguarding that allows bodily autonomy and agency to 99.9% of the population,

---

1 GATE | Global Action for Trans Equality. (2024). *Anti-Gender Movements*. [online] Available at: https://gate.ngo/knowledge-portal/campaign/anti-gender-movements/.

while denying it to the small number of individuals who are trans. Strange, too, how all those would-be safeguarders are shocked by the horrid possibility that a single cis person might set out on a trans journey, yet remain indifferent to the plight of the hundreds of trans people each year forced to endure a cis puberty, a cis existence. More of that later.

I'd like to start with a little about me, jane fae, author of this work, and your guide for the journey on which you are about to embark. I am a writer, sometime journalist – and statistician. I am also, in case you hadn't worked it out yet, a trans woman. Happily transitioned well over a decade ago. Though now, like many trans people in the UK, most unhappily post-transition. Daily, I suffer a crushing awareness of the bigotry ranged against me. I feel its influence within wide swathes of the UK establishment. I am fearful, at any moment, that I might find myself under attack. By a system or by healthcare providers that decide, on a whim, to make it harder for me to access medical treatment. Or loos. Or public spaces.

Conscious, too, each time I step out the front door, that in the present climate I may find myself under literal attack. As has happened to so many other trans people in the UK of late. Mercifully, I have never faced actual assault. I have been threatened, though. More than once. I have had to seek police protection from the haters. I never needed to do that in the before time.

So, do I 'regret' transition? No. Not at all. I do regret living in a world that deems my transition the business of everyone else but me. So many 'experts.'

My past career choices inform this work. As a statistician, and once-upon-a-time scientist, I like to get to the heart of things. I like to clear away the dross, and drill down to what matters in a given field.

Moreover, working at the leading edge of my field, it was increasingly clear that the truth is anything but. Clear, that is. 'Fuzzy' not only has a respected place at the heart of many analytical techniques, it is often the best one can do. So, I know, with a passion, that the moment anyone starts to talk about *the* answer, as though such a thing exists or, if it does, is even knowable, they are talking nonsense.

My natural tendency is to ask questions. That's always easier than providing answers. Still, as a writer, I also have a certain gift. The ability to take, and tell, other people's stories. I enjoy doing this. Moreover, in a world constantly seeking to reduce the spectacular diversity of humankind to cold hard numbers, it is a necessary corrective. The only way to go, if you

...dare to think
Of the greatness, rareness, muchness
Fewness of this precious only
Endless world[2]

Over the years, I have deployed that gift in a variety of ways on behalf of the trans community. As a writer, and before the national press decided that they no longer needed to hear from trans people, I wrote for them. For a while, too, I fended off press

2 Graves, R. (2024). *[minstrels] Warning to Children*. [online] www.Nku.edu. Available at: https://www.nku.edu/~longa/poems/warning.html.

attacks on some of the better known trans-led charities. That is, I advised on how to respond when the mainstream press came calling. Never a pretty sight. For there is nothing fair, factual, or edifying about UK journalists in pursuit of a story. Or, as mostly nowadays, clickbait.

This, in turn, led me to work with trans-led charity Trans Media Watch (TMW). As researcher, as trustee, and - for the last three years - as chair. It is a privilege, and a responsibility, that I do not wear lightly.

I work, too, with TransActual, to whom I owe the publication of this book. Because, at the end of the day, it is the stories that matter. You cannot know a minority – any minority – off the back of cold statistics. People are first and foremost individuals. The joy of people is that no matter who they are, or how they identify, they are diverse. They have lives that are rich, in love, in family, and in friendships.

It is that joy, that diversity that we celebrate whenever we attend a cultural festival. Whenever we march at Pride. For such events are at one and the same time a statement of our existence, a reminder to the world that we are not going away, and an assertion of difference. We are, each and every one of us, unique, and you do us immense disservice when you try to reduce us to some populist cliché.

It is, too, that joy, that diversity, that I seek to celebrate in my own writing. In 2018, I wrote *Transition Denied*[3]. This was the story of a young trans woman – Synestra De Courcy – who tried

3 fae, jane (2018). *Transition Denied.* [online] Jessica Kingsley Publishers - UK. Available at: https://uk.jkp.com/products/transition-denied.

and for a long time failed to receive any support from the NHS for her transition. She died, tragically, just days before a letter arrived inviting her to attend a gender clinic.

The cliché, the easy conclusion, is that these two events were directly related. They weren't. Rather, my own verdict, based on extensive conversations with friends and family of Synestra, as well as access to her own intimate writings, is that Synestra was a complex individual. Intelligent, strong-willed, and dismissive of convention. Yet she faced obstruction and intransigence on the part of those with the power and professional standing to help her. They did not cause her to die. Still, their indifference left its mark; pushed her away from seeking help and support. In 2012/13, she was assaulted, robbed, and raped as she made her way back from a night out to her flat in North London. The police were not helpful. The courts even less so. They decided that while she had been robbed, there was "insufficient proof that the sex was not consensual." Because that's how us trans folks roll, when it comes to sex. We just hand over our money, our keys, and our mobile phone to the first stranger we meet. On the street, at 4 in the morning! Synestra shrugged. She had been reluctant to let the case proceed. Because, this was, after all, "the sort of stuff that happens to people like me." She was right.

Meanwhile, the NHS dithered. For years. Not so much because they weren't sure she was trans. But because admin! It took a visit to her GP, accompanied by an older, wiser hand who knew their way around the system, to get her a referral to the gender service.

Still, she was finding her own way. She was putting her life in order when her own lifestyle – a lifestyle to which the door had been opened in large part because of official indifference – came back and bit her. She died of an accidental drugs overdose in July 2015. I am glad, only, that I have had the privilege of telling some of her story; of setting the record straight as best I can.

And so, *Transitions*. My first thought was that this should be a continuation of the previous work. *Transition Denied II*? The story – or stories – of trans people caught up in the system and failing to progress. A corrective to the misleading narrative pushed by so much mainstream media. The suggestion that a trans person has only to raise their hand for the NHS to roll out the puberty blockers, hormone replacement therapy [HRT], and surgical team. Also, by telling the stories of real trans people, it was to be hoped that this book would act, in part, as inoculation against the dehumanising of us that goes on day after day.

Except, as I began talking to individuals, it became clear that that is only half of it. As you read on, you will encounter individuals who have faced and overcome massive obstacles from family, friends, and medical professionals. They have been denied time and time again. They have been abused and ridiculed for their persistence. In some instances, they have faced actual physical violence.

Despite this, many – most – have come through. They have faced adversity and survived. Or rather, triumphed. As you read this book, my hope is that you will understand that for a trans person, transition, in some form or other, is always going to be preferable to not transitioning.

Yes, there will be times when the road winds back on itself. When temporary progress must give way to greater or lesser setbacks. Even, to that much misunderstood cliché 'detransition,' which is very much not the 'gotcha' that many anti-trans campaigners believe it to be.

Too, there are some who have been lucky enough not to have faced such opposition. They have been supported by family; have had loving spouses and children who have merely shrugged, and carried on. Some even got the new pronouns right first time!

I have not included my own story in this book. My personal experience was bittersweet. Positive, insofar as my then partner was supportive. As she continues to be to this day, almost a decade and a half after she first knew. But sad, because transition also forced me to rewrite my own personal history; to understand that I was trans long before I ever heard that word; and that repressed transness likely adversely affected much of my adult life. If only: the plaint of the 70s child! If only I had known sooner.

Otherwise, this book is simply enough constructed. Three sections worth of background, intercut with three sections of stories. It kicks off with a section all about definitions and terminology. All of the jargon. Plus, a perspective that is less commonly seen in mainstream media, around the 'fuzzy' nature of transness. The second background section provides some history, from Roman castrati to victims of the concentration camps. Some dark. Some light. Yet it got darker still after the fall of the Nazis. For the treatment of trans people was then captured by psychs with attitude. Rogue Freudians. And eugenicists.

In the last section, you will read what has been happening under the most recent Tory government. Because, unless you are directly affected, chances are you have missed a lot of trans-related news. Bad news. Just when things seemed to be getting better, the five years from 2019 to 2024 saw a concerted attack on trans people. On every system put in place to make it possible for us to live straightforward, ordinary lives.

That section was hard to write. In part, because of the feelings of profound gloom it aroused in me. In part, because the last few months of that administration have seen transphobia on steroids. Every week, something awful. So, every time I thought I was done, I needed to update the text with the latest horror.

When it comes to tone and approach, my start point is that I am a journalist and a retailer of fact. Where I state a thing, there will be a cite in the form of a footnote to help you find the basis for any particular assertion. If you don't feel that what is cited is good enough, don't be shy: drop me a line on jane@ozimek.co.uk, and I will do my best to answer all (polite) inquiries. Outside the factual, as you may have noticed, I am opinionated. I have views – strong views – about the chaos wreaked upon the trans community over the past decade, and I am not afraid to say so.

The centre, the focus of this work, lies in the interviews

with a selection of trans individuals at varying stages of their lives. Some very young. Some getting on in years. Some things, they all have in common. Much more is wholly unique to each individual.

Interspersed throughout are poems. Because sometimes it takes the concentration of a poem to communicate the most profound of sentiments. And sometimes, just to lighten the mood. There are a lot of very creative trans folk out there. I suspect that, as a community, we punch well above our weight on the creative front. Let's celebrate that!

And finally, an Afterword. Because, read together, the individual stories highlight patterns. Of treatment. Of attitude. Of motivation. There are lessons to be learnt here. Not least in terms of how trans people feel about how they are treated by the UK establishment. Minor spoiler alert: there is much fear here. Also, anger. Because we are not the demons we have been painted as by the media.

We are ordinary people with one key difference. It does not have to be treated as a major difference. Unless you make it so. Right now, we are enduring terrible times. We are one of the smallest minorities in the UK. Yet judging by the current media moral panic, we are responsible for every ill under the sun. From transing crocodiles (no, really!)[4], to climate change.

It doesn't have to be this way.

---

4 Braidwood, E. (2018). Now transgender people are being blamed for turning fish trans. *Pink News*. [online] 15 Jun. Available at: https://www.thepinknews.com/2018/06/15/now-transgender-people-are-being-blamed-for-turning-fish-trans/ [Accessed 12 Aug. 2024].

Maybe I knew

myself better when I was an infant

--seeing my reflection for the first time

recognizing my body as mine--

than when I was fully grown

developed

against my will

reconciling with the dissonance

between what I wanted to be

and who I was.

The hours I spent looking in the mirror

pretending

I looked like someone else

that I didn't have long hair didn't have breasts

didn't have hips so curvy no men's jeans could obscure them.

Maybe I'll never know how to look into a mirror and see myself

Mirror Stage, by Elias J Donstad

Trans, Transition, Transphobia

When a person says they're trans, they are trans. You don't have to understand. You may never understand. Your job is simply to accept that reality.

Suzanne DeWitt Hall
Author of 'Reaching for Hope'

Concepts, framework, and jargon

It is traditional to begin with definitions. Who am I to buck tradition? Even if many of the challenges that trans people face today can be traced directly to a modern obsession with parcelling everything up into neat little boxes. This is trans. This is not-trans. This is what trans people want, need, demand... This is the prescribed treatment...

I say 'modern', in the sense that discourse 'around' trans people is too often grounded in a certain populist zeitgeist. The idea that things are precisely definable[5]. The supreme overconfidence that assumes humanity can take pretty much any observable phenomenon and explain it. An over-reliance on 'the medical model' when it comes to treating – or 'curing' – everything.

5 To be fair, I blame Aristotle for that. I have written at length elsewhere on the subject. However, since this is a book about trans experience, I shall spare you. This time!

I say 'populist.' Though even writing that, I know that I am generalising; am possibly guilty of the very thing of which I accuse others. Still, the more expert people are in a given field, the less likely they are to claim certainty. Or to assert that they have all of the answers. Across the scientific piste, there is awareness of the limits of research. It took a physicist – Werner Heisenberg – to show how, at the heart of that most absolute of disciplines, lies a fundamental and absolute uncertainty. Schrödinger and his poor put-upon pussycat showed how the very act of observing a thing... changed that thing.

"We'll take that!" piped up social scientists, as they happily coined the 'Observer Effect.' This holds that to observe a thing is not merely to change what occurs, but also to change our perceptions of what occurs. Worse, the very act of measurement tends to change the behaviour of those 'sampled,' leading them to mimic the research findings.

Not quite the same. However, you do not need to be a fully paid-up subscriber to 'anti-trans' ideology, to be aware of a certain slur frequently directed at trans women. Our transition 'reinforces patriarchal ideals of womanhood.' All that wearing of dresses, ultra-femme make-up, and simpering. Slur, indeed. Though not without a kernel of truth. It is a direct consequence of what gender services have, historically, demanded. Those hoping to gain access to the promised land must first prove their worth to a random selection of gatekeepers. They, in their turn – some, at least – will refuse entry to any who fail to conform to *their* ideal of 'womanhood.' Their very particular idea of all the sugar-and-spice essentials you must have.

I was never told to 'wear a dress,' though I know some who have been. Later in this book, you will meet a trans guy lectured for daring to have long hair! Nonetheless, I vividly remember one consultant instructing me on the 'proper way to sit.' If I wished to 'be a woman'! Faced with such intransigence, how would you react? What would you expect a trans person to do?

Meanwhile... "Hold my coat!" went mathematician Richard Bellman. His 'curse of dimensionality' roughly translates into 'the more complex a system, the less knowable it is.' Throw in 'fuzzy set theory' (from statistics); fuzzy semantics (linguistics). Then, even more recently, a re-iteration of the uncertainty principle for social sciences[6]: 'the more popular a particular generalization [...], the less accurate will be the predictions it yields.'

Measurement is not entirely meaningless. Science is not redundant. However, both need to be taken with a very healthy dose of salt, when talking about the human condition. Sadly, the reverse seems more often the case. When it comes to trans people, the last few years have seen an explosion in know-it-all authors, popular press and political soundbitery. A surfeit of best-selling, mostly ignorant books by dubiously qualified non-trans authors. A hundredfold increase, in just ten years, in press articles chewing over the 'trans issue.' The Dunning-Kruger effect - a cognitive bias that leads people with limited competence in a particular area to overestimate their abilities

6 Kashyap, R. (2014). The Uncertainty Principle of the Social Sciences. *SSRN Electronic Journal*. doi:https://doi.org/10.2139/ssrn.2424350.

– is very much alive and well.

Why kick off a book that centres personal experience with an essay on the nature of science? On the meaning of knowledge? It is key. For it frames what follows. So many obstacles are placed in the way of what ought to be purely personal, private decisions. The reasons for this are many, and varied. However, as I suggest below, they have their roots in much wider, misplaced societal tendencies. A belief in 'absolute science.' A delight in boxing things up. The 'medical model.' A sense of what is proper, and therefore right ways to think, act, be. A reliance on 'experts' – that angry, buzzing swarm of sexologists and psychologists who have settled like flies on the backs of trans people - over personal experience and insight.

At its most extreme, this bias shades into effective support for an authoritarian response. Even, eugenics. It makes a rude sort of sense, if you take the paternalistic view. This minority is incapable of knowing itself. It needs wiser heads to decide for it. More widely, as many feminists warn, the direction of travel is profoundly dangerous for all those with 'protected characteristics': women, LGBTQ, those who are disabled. For this approach denies agency to individuals. In its place, a most depressing adherence to conformity and propriety.

Closely related is a touching attempt to explain transness, usually as part of some over-arching theory. Over the years, we've had Freudians claiming we are result of inadequate parenting. We've had politicians claiming it is all the fault of the internet. Or fashion. More recently, we've had claims, from at least one supposedly competent researcher, that trans is 'caused' by porn. What porn? Oh: 'hypno sissy porn'! That's a thing I'd never heard of until I was accused of being addicted to it.

Opposed to this, if less often heard, are voices arguing for a more pragmatic response. We know trans and non-binary people exist; are real. We know what makes our lives difficult. We also know what could improve them. To their credit, there are individuals within the health services of every country prepared to listen. Who would do better if they were given the chance. They are not exactly a minority. Indeed, within gender services, it is likely they are a significant majority. But they have been bludgeoned into silence by the rest. By those with the ear of the establishment, and a touching belief that the future could be better. If only it were more like the past!

"Which of you, if your son asks for bread, will give him a stone?" Ironically, for many in the moral majority, such sentiment is not so much fundamental Christianity, as dangerous wokery. Because, to acknowledge the validity of trans people – to recognise us as anything more than aberration – breaks open the door to a host of unsettling questions. About tolerance. About the role of experts. About 'normality;' and fairness. About medicalisation; and our baffling predilection for psychological charlatanry.

As I may have mentioned, it is dangerous, terrifying, 'to dare to think of the greatness, rareness, muchness, fewness of this precious only endless world.'

Caveats delivered. Now read on.

The view from the cheap seats

As a trans woman, I am frequently assailed by questions. Some serious. Some less so. Some friendly. Some downright rude and impertinent. Another memory from my early days of transition: that time I was invited to an interview by a radio station. Outwardly respectable. The topic? The tragic death of a young trans woman. It went well, for all of five minutes. Until the point when the interviewer swerved and suddenly it was all about me. Had I ever, he wanted to know, 'done it with a man?' I was gobsmacked. Too taken aback to turn the tables which – I kicked myself later – I wish I had.

This is the price of familiarity. Once upon a time, there was a certain mystery to transness. Trans folk existed somewhere outside the realm of normal society. A bunch of 'weirdos' and 'freaks' who underwent operations and procedures that left normal people squirming in leg-crossing embarrassment.

Somewhere along the way, the general public got to grips with the idea that not everyone liked the body assigned to them at birth. They started over here, one side of the great gender/sex divide. Then, after a suitable period of time, and through the application of a variety of eye-watering procedures, they crossed over. He became she. She became he.

In this, the education of the Great British public was much

assisted by informative and hilarious tabloid headlines. 'From hymn to her': a trans vicar. 'There's something amiss about Sir': a trans teacher. 'Sex-swap cop': you get the idea. Rather less funny were the tropes emerging even then, back in the 1970's. As, when trans folk weren't being trivialised, we were all too frequently viewed through a sexualised lens. Nudges and hints of sexual impropriety. Deviance. Fraud and fakery. Holdover, perhaps, from attitudes towards gay people, without legal blessing since 1967, in England and Wales[7]– but still attracting a significant amount of hatred. The language of today's headlines may have improved. The underlying narrative, though, has shifted little.

Still, if you view 'trans' as a simple journey, A to B, you have the tools to deconstruct and –worse – to have opinions about what is in reality a highly individual, personal, and sensitive experience. You can even play it as game, with 'gotchas' built in. Like weaponising 'detransitioners' as somehow proof that transition is a bad idea. Ditto, 'regrets.' I'll return to both those later.

Also, implied by such narratives, is the conceptualisation of trans as some sort of 'choice.' Worse, a fashion fad. It's what the young people are doing. So, clearly, young people need to be safeguarded. And who better to do safeguarding than those self-proclaimed 'experts' in transness? The psychs, and the medical modellers, who first declared transness to be mental

7 But later elsewhere, as homosexuality was not decriminalised in Scotland until 1980, and Northern Ireland in 1982. In addition, the age of consent wasn't equalised until 2000.

illness. That diagnosis has long gone from the textbooks and diagnostic guides. Still, its echo continues to haunt public discourse, with 'sick' and 'diseased' being barbs commonly deployed on social media against trans folk.

For my own part, I am perplexed. It is a startling idea. Experts who had already spent half their career diagnosing, and writing and producing papers, on the basis that trans people were mentally ill, could manage so abrupt a volte-face. Going home from work on Friday night, convinced that trans was something to treat and cure. Back on Monday morning to implement the intense paradigm shift.

I must have missed the bit where they underwent rigorous re-training to bring them up to date.

Definitions, terminology, experience: short hand

From framework to definitions. Though, as I argue in the previous section, too much definition can be a bad thing. The very definition of a 'definition' contains the concept – '*fine*' - of a limit or a boundary. Whereas central not only to much contemporary science, but also to the understanding that trans people have of themselves, is the sense that boundaries, and how we experience them, are fluid. Not fixed at all. Indeed, the more I explore my own identity, as well as how others within the trans community view theirs, the less confident I am with the popular view of trans. A binary A-to-B, either/or version of gender. As you will see in the stories, the real 'defining' characteristic of being trans is some level of trouble with gender. This leads to gender questioning and gender non-conformity. For some, the clear answer is transition. For others it is not. Some may start out by identifying as non-binary. Later they realise they are more 'binary.' Also, vice-versa. Others may understand who they are as early as 4 or 5. Then spend their lives trying to achieve that.

Still, we begin with 'trans'/'transgender': either word works. As formal definition, something broadly along the following lines is widely accepted in the community, and used by a range of trans organisations

> *"An umbrella term to describe people whose gender is not the same as, or does not sit comfortably with, the sex they were assigned at birth. Trans people may describe themselves using one or more of a wide variety of terms including transgender, transsexual, gender-queer (GQ), gender-fluid, non-binary, agender, nongender, third gender, bi-gender, trans man, trans woman, trans masculine, trans feminine and neutrois."*

Nothing will quite capture all of the subtleties that sit behind the trans experience. That, of course, is the rationale for this book. Also, I hope, why you, dear reader, are reading it now. On the plus side, this definition does not include the dread phrase 'born in the wrong body.' That's... part of it. For some trans people. But far from all. Like all simplifications, it has its uses, until such time as critics start to take it too literally.

Contained within it are a number of other terms; some more obvious or self-explanatory than others.

A 'trans man' is someone who is assigned female at birth - AFAB for short - but identifies and lives as a man. A 'trans woman' is the female counterpart to this; someone assigned male at birth - AMAB - and identifying and living as a woman. 'Trans masculine' and 'trans feminine' - 'trans masc' and 'trans femme' for short - are more to do with modes of expression. Although, it depends who you ask. For some these terms are simple modifiers. A declaration, if you like, of how an individual is living their life. 'I am a trans man and trans masc.' Or trans femme. Others use it to denote a direction of travel without assuming a stable endpoint. Often, it is used by non-binary folk to suggest a move towards or beyond an androgynous centre.

'Transsexual' has, historically, been used almost interchangeably with 'transgender.' But beware: it's an 'old school' word, which evokes suspicion and, in some cases, hostility. Because of its clinical nature, and its close association with medicalisation. It is analogous, in many ways, to 'homosexual,' which evokes similar suspicions within the wider gay community.

Yes, you will find it used by different segments of the trans community. Often, though, it is done so ironically. Or as part of a deliberate effort to reclaim slurs. Some argue for its use, since transition is inherently sexual in nature - i.e., not just about gender. One contributor to this book described the word as, simply, 'icky.'

Yes, too, this may seem confusing and perhaps a little unfair. How come *we* get to say things, when you cannot?

Here's the deal: over time, minorities learn through bitter personal experience what the haters call us. We learn that while sticks and stones may be synonymous with inflicting harm, words are not entirely innocent either. Certain words, certain phrases are intended as insult; and they are frequently precursors to violence being aimed in our direction.

So, we fear and avoid those who use such words. It's a matter of self-preservation. Later, though, as a new generation comes through, or an older one grows more confident, we may reclaim some slurs for ourselves. It is how minorities take back control of their lives. Still, just because this or that slur-word is now 'down with the kids,' does not give everyone else carte blanche to use it. This is, at best, faux pas, likely to prompt a shudder of embarrassment in your audience.

At worst, it is provocation. The speaker knows they are skirting the boundaries of politesse. Yet, they prefer to ignore them. A lot of what is characterised in the popular press as 'censorship' is little more than a plea for politeness. Because, faced with a choice of being nice in your everyday interactions, or nasty, why would you ever choose the latter? Sadly, as I highlight below in respect of pronouns and deadnaming, far too many seem to think nastiness is edgy.

I hope I do not need to explain why, for similar reasons,

'tranny' is wholly beyond the pale. The worst. For most trans people the word is synonymous with hate and aggression directed towards them. There are groups who have reclaimed it. This is controversial within the trans community. If you are not trans, do not even think of going there.

The opposite of transgender is cisgender, frequently shortened to 'cis' which is, very simply:

"Someone whose gender identity is the same as
the sex they were assigned at birth."

'Non-trans' is also used. But, less. Despite the near apoplexy displayed by some at being referred to as 'cis,' there is no shade intended. In origin, it is Latin; and just as 'trans' was a preposition used to denote 'on this side of' so 'cis' meant 'on the other side.' After serving for a year as consul in 58 BC, Julius Caesar took up the proconsulship of Gallia Cisalpina. It was so named because it sat *this side of the Alps. It was nearer to Rome than* Gallia Transalpina, where Caesar waged war and for five years pursued a policy of wiping out the transes. Plus ça change!

Is cis, though, a slur? After all, if trans people get to declare what words best describe them, surely cis people – that is, not-trans people – should be accorded the same courtesy? I am tempted. However, the argument seems disingenuous for two reasons. First, there is not a shred of animus embodied in the word. It is just fact. If you accept that trans people exist as a genuine minority, then you need trans-words. Moreover, the existence of trans people implies the existence of non-trans. So, if you are writing about trans people within the wider community, you need words to describe those who are not trans.

What are you going to do? Pepper your prose with 'non-trans' and 'not-trans'? Invent yet another word to descrbe the same thing? Then go round the same circles yet again, as someone decides that 'non-trans' is slur, too? The principle is not analogous. On the one hand, trans people have views on the words used by the wider community about them. Against that, a demand that a very specific and particular antonym be ruled out of existence. Possibly, even, by law. For, some of the wilder anti-trans folks have even claimed that 'cis' is somehow libellous.

The core for that libel, insofar as I can make any sense of it, is that describing someone as 'cis' is to imply that an individual supports and endorses traditional gender roles. Except, it doesn't. It is, very clearly, about how someone identifies.

The second reason that 'cis' attracts a certain notoriety is that using it is, in some small way, a political act. In much the same way as including reference to men *and* women, or the proliferation of *straight or* – horrors! – *heterosexual* as antithesis to *gay* may be classed as political. For until recently, prevailing assumptions, when talking about society, were 'normative'. That is, there is a standard, an average – a norm – that can be used as stand-in for all the wealth and diversity of the whole. Why bother mentioining women when it comes to legislating, when laws apply to all equally? Since 1850, when Parliament passed an Act "for shortening the Language used in Acts of Parliament", until 2007, when it went gender-neutral (again),the only pronoun used in legislation was 'he'. More broadly, why bother mentioning any minority – gay, ethnic, disabled – unless you are discussing that minority?

The downside of this, though, is that every aspect of society is then tailored with the norm in mind. Everything – from seatbelts to kitchens - is designed with the middle-aged, straight, white male in mind. The non-standard, the non-normative, the diverse, are excluded by default. Because, the default is simple: if I don't mention the norm explicitly, the broad assumption is that difference does not matter.

This is what truly lies at the heart of culture war. Is society prepared to acknowledge and accommodate difference? And, beyond that, to recognise that structural advantages exist. Or to deny the importance of inclusion, behind a smokescreen of complaint about 'wokeness', and plausible denial? 'I believe in rights for all'. So the rhetoric goes. Therefore focussing on the rights of any one group is 'intolerant'. Well, no. I believe in universal human rights. But I absolutely believe that if some individuals are disadvantaged, there is moral imperative to help them.

Hundreds of pronouns

Some people also claim to be confused by 'trans pronouns.' Or even reject them on grounds that they do not represent the reality of "biological sex."

Methinks, they do protest a bit too much. In the heightened pre-election atmosphere of 2024, claims were doing the rounds that schools were teaching children that there are 72 genders. Or more. I have never encountered anyone seriously involved in education who has ever taught such a thing. But, but... the 'proof' was in the post. Various folks sent me schematics listing out dozens of flags designed by various segments of the LGBTQ community. These do exist. However, they prove nothing, other than the inevitable human tendency to seek to improve on what has gone before. Often, by sub-dividing one or more categories into ever smaller sub-categories.

Moreover, they are not 'genders.' Many – such as 'lesbian,' asexual and gay – are simply sexualities. They are what they say they are. Badges. Of pride. Of identity. No more; no less.

Besides, I do wonder if those complaining have ever considered the wider world in which they live. Many years ago, I worked for a direct mailing house whose software recognised hundreds of different title variants used by perfectly ordinary cis folks. From Mr, Mrs, Miss, to Professor, Your Excellency and Margrave! As for sub-divisions: last time I looked, Wikipedia was claiming that worldwide there are something like 45,000 versions of Christianity. Do schools teach those, too?

As for that sex/gender thing, it is a major bugbear for the anti-trans. Also, a subject well beyond the scope of this work. Other than to remind folks that biology now acknowledges that sex is far from the straightforward categorisation claimed. Or that there seem no lengths to which they will not go to slur trans people. For, building on unevidenced claims that Olympic boxer, Imane Khelif *might* be intersex, and owner of XY chromosomes, the anti's declared on social media that possessing a uterus - or indeed, being able to get pregnant - did not define one as a woman. Yes, folks: the anti-trans now claim men, too, can get pregnant!

In legal terms, a trans person's sex is given by their gender recognition certificate. Besides, English in general - and Parliament in particular - has never historically required a direct correlation between "biological sex" and pronouns deployed.

So, the main thing to remember about pronouns is that it is polite to use the pronouns that an individual claims as their own. For binary trans folks, that is a simple direct change: he to she; she to he. Want to misgender someone? Well, that is your right. But how would you feel if they misgendered you back? Of course, they shouldn't. Folks need to be better than that.

Getting it wrong - by accident - is no great crime. Though persisting in getting it wrong after being asked nicely might be taken as deliberate rudeness, or even harassment, and treated accordingly.

Singular 'they/them' for non-binary people has a long history within the English language. Pedantic arguments around grammar – outside a linguists' convention – are usually bad faith and – see above – rude.

As for neo-pronouns like 'xe/xem' or 'ze/zem': they exist. They are a rarity in daily use. However, if you encounter someone who uses them, just ask. As for anything and everything to do with pronouns and titles, there is nothing especially difficult about learning how to use them. The question is never really how. It is whether you, as an individual, are prepared to be polite and respect another individual's choice. Or not.

Regret, desistance and retransition

If you spend any amount of time discussing trans people and transition with a non-trans person, the chances are that sooner or later someone will mention regret. Or desistance. Or detransition. Like, 'what happens if you change your mind?' It's a fair question. But one that seems to be deployed disproportionately in conversation with trans folk.

Let's start with definitions. Pretty much all of the words used can be assumed to take their ordinary meaning. It is the logic that follows that is rather more concerning.

Some folks regret choices they have made. Divorce statistics highlight that a great many people regret getting married. So much so that they are prepared to give away a large proportion of their personal wealth in order to reverse that fact. Some people regret having an abortion (16.3%) [8]. Others regret having a hip replacement (between 6% and 30%)[9], or prostate cancer surgery (16%)[10]. In fact, surveys regularly suggest that regret rates for all of these things are significantly greater than the regret rate for transitioning. Yet, it is always transition for which 'regret' – at almost any level – is considered a serious issue.

This also overlooks what is meant by regret and its corollary: desistance, or detransition. First and foremost, regret can be natural response to a complex situation. It is not surprising that individuals who undergo operations that leave them in pain for months after, as they heal, have some regrets. Over time, in many instances, these regrets fade. Other times they last, with individuals declaring they would never have done it had they known the pain it would cause.

I have regrets. I regret being born in a body basically male in shape. I regret the need to transition in order to correct that. I also have occasional more existential regrets, as I consider the forces ranged against me in society. The grand coalition of politicians and media whose single purpose seems, at times, to place obstacles in the way of my enjoying a simple, ordinary life.

---

8 Major, B., Cozzarelli, C., Cooper, M.L., Zubek, J., Richards, C., Wilhite, M. and Gramzow, R.H. (2000). Psychological Responses of Women After First-Trimester Abortion. *Archives of General Psychiatry*, [online] 57(8), p.777. doi:https://doi.org/10.1001/archpsyc.57.8.777.

9 Mahdi, A., Svantesson, M., Wretenberg, P. and Hälleberg-Nyman, M. (2020). Patients' experiences of discontentment one year after total knee arthroplasty- a qualitative study. *BMC Musculoskeletal Disorders*, 21(1). doi:https://doi.org/10.1186/s12891-020-3041-y.

10 Slomski, A. (2022). Some Men with Localized Prostate Cancer Regret Surgery. *JAMA*, 327(1), p.26. doi:https://doi.org/10.1001/jama.2021.23317.

Would I, knowing this, have decided not to transition? No. However bad it gets – and this is a theme repeated many times over in the stories in this book – what I have now is a million times better than before. I think, for the average cis person, that is near incomprehensible. So be it. There are things about my life I regret. Transitioning, per se, is not one of them.

However, that pressure, the fear of how life might be if one transitions, is enough to dissuade some people. For a while. They start out with high hopes of being able to transition. Then they start to encounter opposition. From friends, from family, from work. A couple of years back I reviewed a film, *Markie in Milwaukee*, about an individual detransitioner. They grew up in an evangelical community in the US. On declaring themselves to be trans, their community shunned them. En masse. No-one would have anything to do with them. Not family. Not friends. For a long time, they tried. But unless you have enormous reserves of strength and support, this is a hard hill to climb for the strongest. They desisted.

Another desister I have known personally was in their early 20s when I met them. They began to transition in 2018 and, like their US counterpart, started to encounter resistance from family. Still, the gender service would help. Wouldn't it? In late 2022, they received a letter from the gender service letting them know that they were just getting round to setting first interviews for individuals who entered the system in... 2017! They could expect their first interview – not treatment – in 2024. Or 25. Who knew? This individual desisted. Insofar as they had started on a social transition, they detransitioned.

This, in turn, is a thing regularly weaponised against trans people. If people detransition, it must mean they were not serious before. Therefore, any ask in respect of transition must be resisted. Again, I point to the figures for abortions, for hip replacements, and other procedures. We would be rightly outraged if individuals were not allowed to go forward with any of these without years of psych assessment in advance. It is not how society works. Because, for the most part, we grant agency to individuals and, absent evidence to the contrary, permit informed consent.

Still, not only is the question of regret applied almost uniquely to trans people. This is also an area that abounds with badly designed research and quackery. Any discussion of (de) transition will inevitably throw up, sooner or later, a study from the 90's that claims 80% of trans kids desist. The problem with this? And with a number of similar 'studies'? The definition of what constitutes a trans kid was drawn very widely, by researchers that were at best 'trans sceptic,' if not outright anti-trans. It caught up a lot of individuals who were simply gender non-conforming. Plus, gay and lesbian kids. So, sure: in such a sample, expect a high dropout rate. Because most were never trans to begin with.

Last up, retransition. Again, it is what it sounds like. Many trans people start to transition. They back off when they encounter resistance. Then pick up again later. That makes it hard ever to say with any certainty that an individual has desisted. Because how can you tell, until you know how they lived the rest of their life? Some detransitioners seem to make a thing of it. London lawyer, Samantha Kane famously transitioned, detransitioned and then retransitioned.

Sadly, some do not make it. Like Chelsea Attonley, who I interviewed before her sad suicide. It was always clear she wanted to, needed to transition. But she could not cope with how society wanted to pigeonhole her. After years of transition, detransition and retransition, she took her life in July 2016.

These, though, are the extremes. For others, the journey is more straightforward. However, as you will read in the stories that follow, not every journey is completed in one go. Sometimes, folks need to take a little time out; to rest up before they continue on their way.

When I started T
I knew there would be hair
I knew the places I wanted it
But it turns out; its every fuck-ing where

I have hair on my cheeks
I have hair on my chin
Though I'm sad at the fact
That my tache is a bit thin

I have a skin condition
That makes my arms bare
Same with my legs
But now there's even hair there

I have a hairy belly
It's soft, fuzzy and fine
And it all points to my belly button
For reasons I can't divine

I have little tufts of hair
Growing on my toes
Like little patches of moss
Why? No one knows

I have hair on my chest,
But cognitive dissonance hits
Because "Yes!! I have chest hair!"
But it's growing on my tits!!

As for my crotch
It's gone from shrubbery to thicket
And though it's now 5 times bigger
You'll need a machete to find my clit

My backs getting peach fuzz
My buttocks are too
And in my buttcrack
It's as thick as bamboo

There's hair growing every-where
Well, except on my head,
Where its retreating quite rapidly;
It's moved elsewhere instead.

Hair, by Mal Fox

Transition Stories: I

In this section, you will find the stories of plenty of trans people. Some transitioned. Some on their way to transitioning. Some who have done well. Others who have suffered along the way. Each story is based on an interview I carried out with an individual, and then checked back. Because these are their stories, not mine.

They are a mix. Trans men, trans women, and non-binary people. Young. Old. Lesbian, gay, bi, straight, and ace. People with disabilities and people without. From a variety of ethnic backgrounds. I have sought, in reaching out to individuals, to draw as widely as possible from as broad a range of experience as I could. I even sought out anyone prepared to identify as a 'detransitioner.' One individual came forward. But in the end, no takers.

The one definite exclusion was anyone under 18. Given the tenor of discourse around anything trans-related right now, this felt like a headache I did not need. So, the youngest person included in the interview set is... just 18.

Where possible, I have sought out people who would not obviously be classified as 'activist.' But that is a harder ask than it sounds. The promise to anyone coming forward has been anonymity, should they wish it. For that reason, the majority of interviewees here are referred to by names other than their own. A few – I suspect, the more 'activist' – have been happy to be named. Demanded to be, even.

Others, though, have stepped back. In some instances, after I have done initial interviews. I do not blame them. The reasons they have given boil down pretty much to one single reason. They are scared of the consequences of being outed, even by accident.

They fear repercussions, at work, from family or friends. If you do nothing else on reading this book, think on that. There are members of a minority in the UK who are literally too frightened, in 2024, to own to being who they are.

Of course, in the eyes of the media, any individual who has ever stood on a public platform, stood up for themselves, or just stood up, may be counted as activist and, consequently, fair game. If you have ever complained about anything, from treatment by your GP to the price of fish, you are extraordinary. Because normal people don't complain. Or perhaps they complain, to one another. But they never do anything about it.

Given the state of trans healthcare in the UK, we are all complainers now. All activists. Each and every one of us standing proud and affirming: "I'm Spartacus, too!"

Trans Lives

Anja: A passion for life

Anja is a woman with a passion for life. Passionate European. Passionate about the arts and travel. Happily married. Alright: not quite so passionate about giving away her age, which she describes as "nearer 60 than 50".

Though, courtesy of the special 'trans bonus,' she looks younger. Oh? You hadn't heard of that one?

There is, at least anecdotally, an added bonus to transition: an extra dose of youthfulness, as hormones and HRT put the ageing process on pause. Or for some lucky individuals, send it into reverse.

She is British: born and brought up in East Yorkshire. Her surname, though - Jurgenssen - is her own choice, a name picked deliberately as part of her transition. Anja chose the surname for a range of reasons. On the lighter side, it is reminder of happy memories of travelling across Sweden and Norway. Less light, itis a subtle reminder, based on a character from a Christopher Lambert film, of darker days she never wants to return to.

Anja describes herself as "very out" now. But she has been a long time in arriving, with transition and coming out staggered throughout her life.

When she went for a 'diagnosis,' she owned to having realised at some point in her mid-thirties. Awareness began in

1997 when Anja was involved in a life-changing road accident. She spent 11 days in hospital and left with extra bits of metal to keep various parts together. Whilst not a traditional 'Near Death Experience' (NDE), it was very much a wake-up moment. Whilst recovering, she started to explore computers and the internet, which were then just beginning to get underway seriously. She discovered trans communities online, and this was a game-changer.

Because before then she had known - since perhaps 4 or 5 - that there was something about her that "was not the same as everyone else". However, she admits "I couldn't describe it in terms I understood, let alone explain it to others who wouldn't have understood it anyway." For Anja, the realisation that she was not the only one like her was a revelation. She began to learn about trans history, trans culture, and the pre-colonial acceptance of trans people.

Anja did not exactly grow up in an environment that encouraged 'transness' in any shape or form. Her early education was in a Catholic primary school. There she was treated differently because her parents were divorced. At around 5 years old, she learnt that this was why she was not invited to a classmate's birthday party. Another reason why she spent more time out of school than in.

At around 9 years old (by now the mid-70s) she was aware of the existence of a mildly dodgy class of people that the media called 'transsexual/transvestite.' Sensational headlines about yet another 'sex-change lorry driver/builder/bouncer' and 'how to spot a tranny' made her very aware that acceptance was not the done thing at the time. Whereas ridicule and laughing at trans people very much was.

Mostly, though, she was left to find her own way. As she puts it "I guess some trans people are all about the clothes. That, though, is not really me. I went through a phase of trying to work out which particular 'type of trans' I was. It was all very confusing. I even wondered if being trans meant I wanted sex with men. It didn't take long to realise that that was a pretty definite 'No!'"

What held her back, though, for a long time was shame, and an awareness of what it meant to be openly trans. "At age 15," Anja explains, "I shared with my best (male) friend that I felt more like a woman." It was an awkward attempt to explain something that many trans women feel instinctively: a want, a need to "be with the girls." Not sexually. It was always about socialising. To be 'one of the girls.'

"In that moment, I lost a friend. They decided that being trans meant I wanted sex with men, which in turn equated to being 'a poof.' Later, I tried to rescue that friendship. Some ten years later they did not want to know me. And ten years after that, when they wanted to reconnect, I realised that I didn't want to know them.

Still, it all adds up. Like many trans women, Anja sought to compensate – to bury her transness beneath a veneer of hyper-masculinity. At 16, she joined The Royal Marines Commandos.

Later she joined the police. At 16 she met her first wife, and they moved in together two years later. Marriage followed shortly after.

Jumping ahead, Anja tells how one aspect of 'trans joy' for her was how, on coming out, she met trans women who had pursued similarly macho - and successful - careers as police officers, paratroopers, sub-mariners. There was even a member of the foreign legion, who traced a similar circuitous route. Because, for the first time, she was able to tell herself: "It's not just me, then!"

It was a long slow journey, and not without its share of tears along the way. Anja's parents divorced when she was 5 and, as for many trans people, the process of coming out to parents was both important and hard.

Her father, she tells me, is 'a weather-beaten, salty old sea dog' who has lived more time on the world's oceans than ashore. When she told him in 2000, his initial reaction was outrage. And yet... Two years later, she tells me, "He became one of my strongest supporters." Her mother, on the other hand, has become much more distant. "She is OK with it; but still, she struggles."

Sometime later Anja divorced, and being trans was a large part of this. So, she limped on into the noughties.

Not being able to be open is awful and being rejected by a partner is awful. In 2000, she went to see someone known to be a trans-positive therapist.

His initial assessment report, she describes as being

"devastating." It talked of consequences for her in terms of the 'loss to this person in social standing, career, and family.' A year or so later, she returned as Anja. En femme. When she walked in, he was shocked, surprised. Anja explained her reasons for returning female-presenting, and his reaction was very different. Contrite, even. He apologised for 'not having been very kind.'

Still, it was in many ways a wasted decade. She abused alcohol; suffered from poor mental health and became overweight. She was on a self-destructive path, and she didn't care anymore. For a while, even, she put her transition on pause because "everything was falling apart." She worried that medication was part of the problem.

Then, slowly, things began to change. She reconnected with a woman she had known earlier in her life. They married and, for a while, Anja reverted to "the male me." Because it felt so overwhelmingly difficult to change. Because of the positive reinforcement that came with hyper-masculinity. Because she was afraid of losing everything again.

This time, though, it was different. She had a supportive partner – one who joked about keeping the spare bits post-op (this, I can confirm from personal experience, really is a thing that is offered; although in the NHS, this is not a request that will be agreed to, nowadays).

She could not ignore her gender issues any longer. She had reached a point where she felt she no longer had anything to lose, and she was no longer worried about others pointing and laughing.

It was time to get a referral. Her regular GP was not enthusiastic, but in 2013, a locum referred her to the Laurels gender identity clinic, in Exeter. It took a year for them to assess her. Another 6 months to write up a report and, crucially, recommend HRT.

Still, one obstacle remained. Her regular GP said, "I'm not treating you."

'This is a 14-page document! I haven't got time to read this. I don't know how to treat you for this so I can't treat you.'

It was left to Anja to explain NHS policies; how 'shared care' worked; and the rest. Eventually, her GP, on the verge of retiring, went "Sod it! I'll do it." The rest is history, as Anja now has a named GP who is "brilliant when it comes to trans healthcare."

Since then, she has gone from strength to strength.

She has been living full-time as a woman since October 2022. But by then, it was hardly a secret. Taking part in a national project for Police Now, aimed at breaking down barriers between police and marginalised communities, she reckons she came out to 120,000 officers in one go, one of whom was her former Boss! "Everyone," she smiles, "knows about Anja!"

Her daughter has been supportive, and Anja was moved to tears when she said, 'One day, no one will have to come out and honestly, it's not a big thing.'

Relations with her son remain more difficult - though not because she is trans.

She was recruited into her current role, with the OU, as herself. No more hiding! At the time of writing, she is a co-chair of the trans staff association, she says of the OU, "They are the nicest people ever."

She knows the difficulties that some people face in coming out. She is well aware of anti-trans hostility. So far, though, she has been fortunate. She doesn't feel discriminated against. No one has 'had a go.'

She drinks in the same pub she always has, and goes to the same chip shop, takeaways, and shops, with no issues. Though she has little doubt some do talk behind her back. There are looks; and double takes. Although mainly at remembrance services when she wears her medals. Sometimes she has a sense that people want to say something, perhaps even positive, but they hesitate.

Part of that, she believes, is because she is so happy. "I used to wake up thinking 'here we go again.' Now there is a simple joy to being able to get up in the morning and be me. Just hearing my name is wonderful, constant affirmation of who I am. I even have mirrors in the house, now!"

"If you walk in somewhere, walk in like you own the place, that usually works."

For Anja, handing in her card to the boys' club has been a real change.

At the outset, she was not sure about surgery. "It was too big a question." Now, assured of the help and support of her spouse, she feels it is the right thing for her. But there is a lot more to get done first, including making sure they are financially secure first.

She worries about pain after surgery. Otherwise, her only regret is putting herself into a prison of her own making for so long, through the fear of how she would be treated after coming out.

We end with a brief moment of philosophy. "Transition," she muses, "is like a train journey.

"Some head for platform 1 and know exactly where they are going. It's Express all the way. One friend took this route. She sold everything, did two jobs, and just saved and scrimped every penny to get through the process as quick as possible.

"Others like talking, looking out windows, meeting new people" and enjoying the journey.

It's been a long journey. But Anja is getting there.

April: A breath of fresh air

Within the trans community, there has long been a debate about 'passing.' Is it better to slip under the radar of friends and colleagues? To pass through life unnoticed and undetected? Or, particularly for trans women, is being invisible - a requirement originally imposed by non-trans medics - a burden? A buying-in to deep-rooted sexism within society. Is it a bad thing to wish to be ordinary?

For April (not her real name) ordinary has been a blessing. She goes to work, does her job - something technical and "very boring" - goes home, sleeps. She is mostly 'stealth,' which means very few beyond her immediate circle knows she was ever anyone other than she is now. Her story, uncontroversial, not greatly troubled by setbacks and social rejection, is what many would choose if they could. It is no different, no more startling than a million stories you might hear from any other 30-something woman living in the Home Counties.

Still, certain things needed to happen to make it so. To begin, like many trans folk, April knew early that 'something was up.' She says: "About 13/14 I was desperately trying to figure it out. It was a feeling that clawed constantly at my brain. There was some sort of disconnect between me and my body. My body felt not right; and over time, this just got more and more obvious.

"I didn't instantly understand this as 'being trans.' I was at a comprehensive school, in London, where no-one ever talked about this stuff.

"But I knew about the existence of trans people and it resonated. I understood that this is what I am. This is what I have to do."

Still, this insight brought a lot of anxiety. She was a young teenager, still very much subject to parental control. She expected disapproval, especially from her dad, who had expressed negative views about transness in general. In time they adjusted. At the outset, though, the fear of rejection was very real.

She was 14/15 when she told her mum, and had no idea what to expect. April hoped she would help get her a GP appointment to talk about it. But she blanked her; did not acknowledge.

"Maybe," April speculates, "she was just processing it; wanted nothing to do with it."

Still, to April's surprise her parents eventually came to terms with who she was. Though her younger sister took a while to get used to her.

For April, the best outcome would have been to go through the system officially. But the wheels of the gender service grind exceeding slow.

At 16, she started on hormones, which she obtained through the grey market. She was also lucky that when, eventually, she got to see her GP, they were happy to give her a 'bridging prescription.' Many won't. They also referred her on to the adult service. By then, though, she had already taken matters into her own hands and seen a private specialist on Wimpole St.

She transitioned socially (changing name, style of presentation, etc.) at 18. Her primary concern at this point was university. She wanted to go on to university after college, but didn't want to until everything was done. "If I couldn't finish it all, I think I would have postponed university until it was sorted. It felt like everything was fraying, crumbling. I felt stuck.

"Looking back now, I wonder if was the most mature approach."

Her fears, though, were unfounded. In the end, she obtained surgery privately, in the UK. Parents helped with the cost, as did an inheritance, from her grandma. She was 19.

Since then, she tells me, she has not looked back. "For a while it was exciting – a sense of... 'yes, let's go.' Now, it just feels like living my life. Ordinary. Gender stuff is done.

"Being trans does not get in the way. But I don't really talk about it, with colleagues or people I meet.

"Sometimes, it can be awkward if I tell people. Occasionally, people have drawn back, and I never can be sure if that is why. I had one friend who reacted very strangely. I told him some time before I started to transition. He seemed to think it was a joke. Then as I started to put things in place, he disapproved. A lot. One time we were out, he started walking way in front, trying to distance himself from me.

"He'd never done that before. He was embarrassed by how I looked."

"Now I have a relationship with a young guy. Telling him was 'interesting.' We met at work. I didn't want to tell, but I told him by text. He disappeared for the weekend; didn't say a thing.

"The following weekend he was back. He'd done some thinking and was prepared to give it a go. I guess I challenged his sexuality a little. For him, I was the unknown, and he had to get through some kind of barrier to be OK with it.

Any regrets? None!

As for the clothes? They have nothing to do with it!

Jake: Gaslit and denied

If ever you want to know how the current system dismisses and gaslights trans people, just ask Jake.

Jake is 31 and "trans masc". He used to say he was "trans

male" and still uses 'he.' Though now he considers himself to be more gender non-conforming. When it comes to transition, though, he feels the label is less important than goals. He is not a fan of rules for 'how you must be.'

He tells me: "I don't know where I picked up what trans was. But when I was in primary school, maybe year 1, I remember saying 'when I grow up, I am going to be a boy'. I also picked my name. I'd like to have been 'Jay' – loads of blokes in my family have names starting with 'J' – but sadly someone else got there first.

Then life got in the way. Nothing much more happened until I was 19. Then, a friend asked what I would have been called if I were boy. That triggered a memory.

"It felt a bit like being hit round the face. Because it wasn't a gradual realisation, but a remembering. Because I had known in the past.

"Then everything fell apart for a while. Because no way was I going to ignore it. I needed to get my head around what came next. But I had partner issues. The first did his best to help.

"But past issues, on both sides, made it difficult. His experience with his mum, who was disabled, meant he was used to having to do things for people when they couldn't. Not controlling. Rather, he tended to take on responsibility. At the same time, I was unstable, and at risk. So, he took over trying to keep me going.

"I, in turn, was dependant on him at a really bad time. Though it got worse later with all the nonsense thrown at me by my hospital. But he didn't create the situation. He was wrong when he told me: 'You're not going to do this. This is a bad decision. You need to take time to think it over.' Still, the net effect was to add delay.

"We broke up. I still knew I was trans. But I did listen to him to the point of trying to carry on without transitioning. That's how the next boyfriend happened. Except, he was straight and had no wish to stay with a guy. I didn't hold that against him. We both knew from the start that was possible. He was hard to handle when I first came out. But we're still friends." Still, it impacted Jake's studies. He went to Bangor to study marine biology. He finished his first year. Then, after retaking year 2, he dropped out. It was at this point, aged 20, that he came out.

But Jake has had mental health issues since at least 16. He is also autistic, with a tendency to hyper-focus. Both labels have been used at different times by 'gender experts' to dismiss what he was saying.

As a young child he was bad at social stuff. He had anxiety around people in general. A major issue was difficulty in understanding what other people mean. "Things other people think are normal I don't. Sometimes I have an idea and I have to ask others how it is that the idea is what it is. When it is something only I understand, it's difficult. They want you to accept what they say; but they won't just accept what you say.

"So, their problem is my problem; and my problem is my problem!

As example Jake points to his hair. It is long. One psychiatrist told him: 'you have to cut your hair to be a man.' At the time, Jake was into heavy metal. Still is. "I know a lot of men with long hair. One of them was sometimes with me when they said that!

"So, this psych is telling me men can't have long hair. But they are sat in a room with a guy with long hair. They just kept insisting. They refused to say 'why.' They also kept saying I did not have gender dysphoria. It was 'just' body dysmorphia. What was he going to do about it? Nothing. Again, though, he refused to explain.

After coming out, Jake found he'd traded one abusive, controlling relationship for another. Because, back then, in Wales, access to the Gender Identity Service required a psych referral. Only, a lot of Welsh psychs seemed to enjoy acting as gatekeepers.

Because he was already accessing mental health services, he asked for a referral. 'Think about it,' they told him. Jake followed up: sometimes two years elapsed between appointments. A new therapist looked into his notes, found nothing had been done. But he wanted to wait a bit longer as well. It was all 'too soon.'

So, Jake changed therapist. Over 8 years a procession of therapists got in his way. Some just refused outright. They weren't convinced. One told him that if he did not want 'everything, all at once,' then they wouldn't refer. This is throwback to the idea that there is just one 'proper' way to do trans.

Only, Jake did not want testosterone. Because he sings; and

he did not want to ruin his singing voice. Logical, eh? Not for these psychs. One even claimed – not once but three times – that he had made a referral that was rejected. It turned out he never did.

At this point, Jake was suffering a lot from depression and anxiety. He says: "There was nothing I had control over. My life was on hold. Everything had to wait. It was very difficult, especially when I had to see them. Part of the problem was social transitioning with no way to do so physically.

"Every time I went back, I got worse. I attempted suicide. I remember a lot of ideation, and self-harming. These were coping methods. Often, I left sessions suicidal, not just generally depressed.

"I learnt never to go to an appointment unaccompanied. Because there were bridges in the vicinity; and I could have been in a suicidal mood when I left.

One therapist brought up a load of tenuous stats, about regret. He was adamant that Jake would regret transition. He accepted that Jake was at risk; and he (the therapist) appeared unconcerned about increasing that risk.

Another said he was not autistic. However, assessment since then confirms that Jake is very high on the autism scale. Even Jake's decision to be accompanied became an issue. Because the psychs would talk to the person who came with him, and not him. Sometimes, they even wrote down what the companion said, and not what Jake told them. Along the way, one of them ventured a diagnosis of BPD.

"This stemmed from a comment the person with me had made. I contradicted it. Yet they used his input to try and label me. Thankfully, that is why I was able to get it struck out later. Because it was so clearly not true. They'd just made it up." About the only plus to being accompanied was that someone else got to see what was happening. As one put it: 'The psych is just misogynist. You're a woman and you don't know what you're going on about, basically.'

He knew how damaging it was because his GP, who he describes as "brilliant," kept chasing them. One time, he went for a medication review. The psych refused to discuss anything except why Jake was trans. Result: no review! Even though that was the reason he was there.

They, though, preferred to blame any issues on Jake.

Every time Jake saw them, they challenged him about being trans. One demanded that he explain 'what makes you a man?' The question came with a rejection of Jake's sense of self, continual belittling, and a large dose of 'that doesn't count.'

Not surprising that Jake says now: "I dreaded going back. I hated it. I would rather die now than go back!"

Or more positively (I think): "The entire health board needs burning down and starting afresh. It is a massive board that cannot control itself. It's a disaster that needs sorting out, from the ground upwards. We need a completely fresh canvas to start over. But until we stop under-funding and start paying for good people, it will carry on failing."

Sure, I hear the commentators revving up: this is just one

personal view. Though it is also the view of the Welsh Public Services Ombudsman[11]. They reviewed this case and, in 2021, decided that the Health Board failed in its treatment of Jake. They had decided he was not trans, and as result would not refer him to a gender clinic. Although one did 'seek informal advice from the gatekeeper'.

They also wondered if there had been breaches of both the Equality and the Human Rights Acts. This, though was beyond the scope of the review. As for going to court, Jake did not have the energy. Ashe put it, "I just wanted a meaningful apology. Something more than 'We're sorry you feel we did something wrong', which they eventually conceded."

Too, in 2020, all changed. Wales adopted a new route for referrals to gender clinics. As England put in place a few years previously, you no longer needed to go through a psychiatrist. Jake got a referral from his GP. Better still, because he had been waiting so long, this was backdated by four years. So, now he was at the front of the queue.

There, a therapist acknowledged what the Welsh psychs had denied for 8 long years. Jake was trans. They talked about what that meant to him. Was he trans or non-binary? They added a non-binary support worker to the mix to help him explore. But they were not insistent. This was not the gatekeeping to which he had become used.

---

11 Ombudsman Wales/Ombwdsman Cymru (2021). *Clinical Treatment in Hospital: Betsi Cadwaladr University Health Board.* [online] https://www.ombudsman.wales/. Available at: https://www.ombudsman.wales/findings/appointments-admissions-discharge-and-transfer-procedures-betsi-cadwaladr-university-health-board-2/.

Besides, Jake was not too bothered by labels. He was clear as to the outcomes he wanted, and that was what mattered. A mastectomy followed shortly after. Again, he has nothing but praise for the surgical team. "They were brilliant!"

Because once the NHS puts its mind to getting a thing done, it usually does it well.

They set out options. Jake didn't have many questions. After all, "I'd been thinking about this non-stop for 10 years. Been saving up because was afraid I'd have to go private."

Better yet, the op came as pleasant surprise. "I went into hospital for a pre-op appointment. When I left, I had a date for surgery. My guess: they had a cancellation.

All this has lifted Jake's mood and mental health massively. "In part, that's because I never have to go back and see those people again. Because they always made my mental health so much worse."

As soon as he was on a real list, waiting no longer mattered.

"Now I rarely self-harm. It used to be constant. No more. In the same way, I have much less negative ideation.

"I am seeing a therapist now. They reckon what went before was conversion therapy. It never occurred to me that could happen on the NHS. I never imagined that being sent by my GP to sort out mental health issues could lead me there. Yet instead of dealing with my mental health, it was all about 'you're not trans'."

Jake is not currently planning to have further treatments. His singing voice is a major support for him. He is also not keen on losing his hair.

But he is a realist. There might be a time when they feel right. At some point he likely will have a hysterectomy. For now, though, he is taking a well-earned breather

He still has depression. But the outlook is so much more positive. According to one friend: 'Jake is happier than she (sic) ever was.

"I got my very first job, at age 30. I started volunteering at a local wild life trust. Then, after three years they found enough money in one of the projects to take me on. It's part-time; just 7 hours a week. But it gets me of the house.

"I'm also getting up every day. Downstairs, too. That's a change from ten years ago when I took refuge in my bed, with just the odd night out socialising. I am in a better place all round."

He is also now a trustee of local mental health charity Amser I Siarad.

His family are supportive. "My parents understood and were not at all surprised. Likewise, my sister. My (grandmother - mum's side - had a dream about me being a man the night before my parents told her I was trans. Sadly, my other gran had late-stage dementia. All this would have confused her. So, we haven't told."

Otherwise, "I'm not in a relationship right now. It's just all complicated by being so in-between and non-conforming. Most people who are into men are into a manly man. Not someone in between.

"But it's not a major goal. If it happens, it happens. And for now – at long last – I am doing OK on my own."

Kim: Loud and Proud

"I am very out. Loud and proud!" That's a bold claim. But Kim's story bears witness to the difference just one person can make. If they are prepared to take a risk.

She is a trans woman. 52 this year, and a Brit abroad. She lives in Taiwan, for reasons that will become obvious. However, when we spoke, she was back in Torquay, visiting friends and family.

Like so many I have spoken to, she knew early on that 'something was different.' She tells me: "It was summer, 1977, and I was about 4. I went into a corner shop with my pocket money. Queuing. The man in front turned and said – pointing to me, 'Let the little girl go first.'

At that age I was small with curly hair and fine features." I burst into tears. 'It's not my fault,' I shouted, 'that I'm not a girl.' At 11, testosterone hit. Such a cruel poison in my bloodstream!

"As a young adult in the 80' and 90's, I did not have the language, or the knowledge, to comprehend who I was. I had a strict Catholic upbringing and went to a Catholic boarding school - Prior Park College in Bath. It was an all-round bad experience."

We digress briefly. Back in the 80s, I lived in Bath. May even have given a talk about politics at Prior Park. My memory is hazy. Nothing LGBT-related. Though strange, nonetheless, to think our paths might have crossed so long ago.

Kim continues: "For a while, I thought maybe I was a gay man. I was comfy with the gay community in London. As label, though, it never quite fitted.

"Too, as I got older, I felt that something was dreadfully wrong. Whatever it was lay buried under layers upon layers of psychological archaeology.

"When it came to sex, the last thing I wanted was to penetrate in any fashion. As a teenager, even though I didn't know I was trans, I remember saying over and over 'I don't know how to do this.' I am bisexual. I enjoy relationships with men and with women. Though when it came to women, what I craved was to be part of 'female society.'

"By my late 20s, a pressure was starting to build. Everything about who I was felt wrong. There was dysphoria, too. It felt terrible. I would look at my reflection in the mirror and feel physically sick."

By her 30's, Kim was working in offshore construction - a 98% male industry. It wasn't quite the plan. She'd started out in marketing and business intelligence. Then, in 2008, the financial crash hit. A lot of small businesses went bust. She lost everything, and needed a new career. Perhaps it was not entirely surprising that she followed in the footsteps of so many trans women before her and opted for a hyper-masculine role. To cover up. To hide.

She had enough money left for a Master's degree, which is

how she ended up in this area. Her aim, initially, was to sink into obscurity. A scientist and technician overseeing aspects of offshore construction.

She worked on offshore construction ships building oil and gas fields in over a dozen countries from the Pacific to the Atlantic, the North Sea and up in the Arctic Circle. Then offshore windfarms. This took her around the world. Stopping off in ships in, she jokes, "all tourist destinations," because industrial ports are not the most attractive of places. This, in turn, started to open her eyes to possibilities.

Her 30s were also a decade of torment. Over identity. By 2010 it was obvious something was wrong. But the precise shape of that wrongness was still deeply buried. Talking now, Kim tells me: "It is very hard to go back to that period. I was married. To a woman. Our sexual relationship broke down completely. I just withdrew. I couldn't focus on loads of stuff in my personal life. My blood pressure was through the roof: 240/140. I was very overweight. Depressed.

Through all this, Kim recalls one bitter sweet moment of insight. "I had been talking about wanting to express myself in a more feminine way. Then, on my 40th birthday, my partner surprised me by recommending I try a trans dressing service.

"She meant well. The experience, though, was horrid.

"A woman did my make-up and it was monstrous. Slutty! I found the least slutty clothes I could and looked in a mirror. It was horrible. Still, I saw some glimpse of defiance in the eyes. Inside, I was saying 'this is me. You may never have seen me before. But this is who you are. You can bury me back inside. But this is who you are.

"It was sad. It was also a profound moment of insight. Because I knew then that this thing I kept inside was not the same as men dressing up as woman for sexual pleasure.

By now, though, Kim was starting to take back control of her life. She read up on the subject, and designed her own route.

She spoke to different GP's. One - a woman -told Kim to 'man up.' She also asked if she had tried Viagra!

Another, in Plymouth was little help. No support. No information. Not terribly interested, because she was abroad so much.

"In my early 40s I tried oestrogen for first time. Gender GP helped with that. Though I also had to do one session with a therapist. That was mostly by email.

"Within days of starting, my blood pressure was back to normal. My depression disappeared. My weight started to return to a healthier level. Unfortunately, after around two months, someone came across an email from a pharmacist. They told. The news spread quickly around my ship, and the weeks that followed were brutal. Insults. Practical 'jokes.' I'd wake up in morning to find a picture of a 'chick with a dick' on my cabin door. I was pushed down stairs. Slapped on my ass. Punched. There were other attacks. But I was a freelancer, dependent on the good will of my clients. A freelancer who complains doesn't get phone calls for more work.

"There was no route to handle it except to endure in silence.

"So, yet again, I buried who I was. I stopped taking oestrogen. Hello, depression, my old friend!

"Of course, it couldn't last. Being on oestrogen just felt right."

I nodded. One of the markers of being trans seems to be how one responds to specific hormones. Like many a trans person before me, I have often speculated that there is a fast, simple way to tell if someone is trans. Just give them the hormones. And if they thrive, the chances are: they are.

At this point, though, Kim was still trying to go slow. "I was just going to take oestrogen as a medicine. I didn't believe I'd ever pass. Social transition was the last thing on my mind. I told myself I could continue pretending to be a man.

"Then, I was on a ship in Nigeria. We were only meant to be there for 6 weeks. But we ended up stuck for about 4 months. I ran out of hormones and it was a nightmare. Hot flushes. Mood swings. Difficulty sleeping. My weight ballooned.

So, it was back to the HRT. This time, my body started to change. I stockpiled a 6-month supply of tablets, to ensure I didn't run out again. It was challenging. But I managed.

"I'd been on oestrogen another 6 months, a year, when I started a job in Taiwan. This was about three years ago, shortly before Covid arrived. I didn't dare transition socially. So, I wore androgynous clothing. But no make-up. Short hair. Still hiding."

If you are a trans woman, though, you can only hide for so long. "One day I realised my breasts were too big. I spent ages minimising. But I couldn't hide any more.

"I went shopping for a bra!

"In the store, the assistant, a Taiwanese woman, took me into a changing room. It was the first time I saw self with tits in a bra. I started crying. I said: 'I can't hide this any more.'

"I then spent the rest of the day in the store, just buying clothes. Then make-up. Then a crash course in make-up. I went back to my hotel and the best part of 200 incredibly macho workers. The rest of the weekend, I spent locked in my room. Practicing. Monday morning, I put on my clothes, my make-up, and went down to breakfast.

"I was nervous as hell. As you can imagine, the whole room silent. Then some started laughing. I found self in a queue with everyone just staring."

This was a turning point. It was not, though, without consequences.

"Over the next 3 to 6 months, I was on the receiving end of hundreds of verbal assaults. There were dozens of actual assaults. Two serious sexual assaults. The industry closed ranks and excluded me."

As one door closed, though, another opened. "My only way back in was by doing talks. On technical issues that affected the industry, but people were too scared to speak of in public. On government regulations. In some quarters, I was branded a real trouble-maker trans woman.

"Elsewhere, I started getting invited to speak. A lot of invites to speak at senior level. Some big companies have asked me to present what it is to be transgender in their industry and to explain how, why they need to support. Other companies and even government departments wanted to gain more insight into the technical issues.

"Because before I came out, there was next to no visibility for LGBT people. Since, though, I have had 100s of people getting in touch. That includes gay men, as well as trans women who thought they could never come out."

She no longer has issues with people knowing. Pride week in Taiwan is in October and Kim has been asked to speak at events there. She has had a lot of people contact her, and she wants to be as much help to those coming up after as she can.

"It's been hell getting to where I am."

That includes yet more drama when she underwent surgery in Barcelona. Gender affirmation. Facial feminisation. She went private. This was the only realistic avenue to complete a full transition in a reasonable time. Though the cost took literally every penny saved up over years. Because the total cost for the surgeries and treatments was in the region of £100,000. Despite it emptying out the coffers, Kim says: "It was worth it a hundred times over. Even though I struggled financially for several years afterwards."

Yet after so long at odds with her own body, Kim has finally found peace. On a community forum about a year ago, she was curious. She started a thread asking whether: 'After surgery did anyone feel like they had a phantom penis?'

Kim says: "I can't even remember having had the other 'stuff,' now. My body just feels natural. Though I have not been with men since my surgery."

Perhaps, she is taking the advice of her gran, 97. Both mother and grandmother were positive when Kim told them. Her gran, though, asked if she dated boys or girls. Kim said she wasn't interested in the person's gender; more in the quality of the relationship. Her gran replied: "You need to find a good woman. It's easy to find a good woman. It's not easy to find a good man."

Kim doesn't have children. This, she puts down to her anger when going through male puberty when she realised she could never have children of her own. She was also estranged from one family member. A lesbian who, according to Kim, has a great deal of self-loathing. "Sadly," she adds, "she died from an aggressive cancer before there was any chance of a reconciliation."

But in the end, she is optimistic. "It's getting better. Change is possible. And I am a tough bitch and ready to give as much as it takes to get there."

August: Half and half and happy

Society likes folk who fit in. That can be an issue when you don't quite match social expectations. Or a challenge. August decided to pick up the gauntlet. So far, they appear to be winning!

When I spoke to them, they owned to being 22, and "trans masculine, somewhere in between non-binary and a trans man." When it comes to pronouns, they are happy with he/they. And – music to my ears! – they are studying classics, at Worcester College, Oxford. For some reason they have never quite understood, it is a four-year degree.

An extra year of university. On the plus side, that gives them space to explore topics in greater depth. Right now, they are comparing how trans people are presented today - and 2000 years ago. Their focus is on a fascinating sect, the Galli, whose priests devoted themselves to the goddess Cybele. Also, castrated themselves, and wore women's attire.

Whether the Galli genuinely represented an early manifestation of transness is subject to much debate. What is clear, though, is that they led many - including the Roman poet, Catullus - to question gender roles.

For August, asking questions comes naturally. Though they admit that others might have had difficulty with some of their answers. "That," they told me, "Is what happens when you try to explain a thing that is part of lived experience. It is just harder."

They have autism and adhd. This prompted them to question some basic assumptions. They tell me: "I never really understood gender roles. Some years back I started asking questions. I may even have begun asking about gender. But everything got attributed to autism. It was gaslighting. That, and a refusal to listen.

"Still, I didn't think at all about gender when I was going through secondary school. That was lucky, because I am not sure I could have coped at that time.

"University, though, gave me more space. End of first year, I started to think about gender. What made sense for me? I realised I could carry on living as a girl. But that meant being unhappy. Or I could adjust. I gave up trying to stop myself.

"I found a place in London that offers 10 sessions talking with a trans person. That allowed me to explore. To get help. I did that for a term, before I started to get out there. It didn't take that long, as once I started to think about it, everything fell into place quite quickly.

"I surfaced memories from years previous. At one time, I remembered, I was obsessed with the idea of being someone's best man at a wedding. Too, a friend of a friend knew a trans guy who became pregnant. I could not stop thinking about that. Now, I understand that this was who I desperately wanted to be.

"I spoke to a guy who set out a list of things for me to do. Together we identified key tasks. It was helpful, even if not meant to be therapy."

August talks about presenting "half and half." They do not feel more one thing than another. "I still wear female/feminine clothing at times. It depends on the day, and whether I wish to present more masc or more femme.

"It's a mix that works for me."

As far as friends and family are concerned, it is no big deal. "Everyone knows. I only really interact with LGBTQ people; and the vast majority are fine with how I am.

"Most friends use 'he/him.' Parents use 'they/them.' I think, in their heads that can be 'woman-lite.' It allows them to still see me as 'she.' Whereas, if they said 'he/him' they would have to change. For them, this is the least effort. They are very scared of me changing further. They are scared of hormones or surgery.

"By the time I came out to my parents, I'd already told pretty much everyone in uni. I'd also changed my name legally. They struggled. With my identity. With being 'left behind.' I doubt they would have tried to stop me. But I knew they would react negatively.

"It felt like my mum was worse. But then, she thinks it's positive to put all her feelings 'out there.' She made snide remarks. Like, 'I thought I raised you to think women could be anything, why would you do this?'

"I see less of an emotional face from my father. His attitude is 'It's fine.' Equally, though, if he had issues, he'd be 'It's fine: don't tell the child.'

"As far as I am concerned, I've not done HRT or surgery. Yet. I'm not planning on surgery. Not expecting to go that road. Transition is about being me; being my correctly gendered self.

"But I have time. I'm OK with where I am now. If... when... that changes, I will change, too."

August says there have been no issues with any professors. A simple email took care of change of name and pronouns. The response, by and large, was 'cool.' They also now have a number of trans tutors.

In fact, about the only time they have run into problems was when they decided to stand up for their principles. In 2023, a prominent 'gender critical' academic was booked to speak at the Oxford Union. August is an exec member of the LGBTQ soc. They put out a statement saying they wished the invite had not been made.

The academic posted about that on twitter. The society found itself on the receiving end of a pile-on. 10,000 comments and a load of hate. Committee members were doxxed. That is, their personal details – including addresses – were made public. The society President also received a death threat.

It was, August admits "a difficult time. Overall, though, it was good. There were counter-protests. We organised a petition asking that she not be platformed. A load of colleges joined us in signing that. Then I ended up helping to organise the first trans pride in the city."

Not everything is plain sailing. Still, with a little optimism, August is working their way through. Because… why wouldn't they?

Adam: Agender, unrecognised

As a young adult, Adam already has a wealth of academic achievement under their belt.

Starting at Coventry University, their background is in politics, history, sociology, linguistics, literature, and philosophy. Since then, xe[12] spent a year at the University of Luxembourg where xe founded the first LGBT+ student association in the country. Proudly, xe tells me: "It is still going to this day. And it has also won national awards.

12 a gender-neutral neo-pronoun.

Now xe's at Queen Mary University of London, researching a Master's in International Relations. "The focus," xe explains, "is about applying critical theory to world politics. Here, postcolonial, feminist, and queer theories.

Adam identifies as non-binary, agender. Pronouns are they/them. Or xe/xem. Xe describes xemself as a social activist, combining creative and academic. Xe has spent the last 7 years creating 'systemic change' through Transcribe Birmingham, in the Midlands and beyond. Xe was also involved in founding a number of organisations, including Trans Pride Birmingham.

If that all sounds a bit 'privileged and woke,' think again. According to Adam, "A lot of what I do, including coming to terms with my own identity, is to do with adversity and marginalisation. I was in and out of care for much of my childhood. I was moved around a lot in England and Wales. At one point I was placed back with my biological family. When they learnt that I identified as gay, they gave me an ultimatum. 'Not under this roof. Or get out'."

This added to an already long and difficult history. There were reasons why Adam went into care in the first place. So, xe decided it was better for xyr mental health to get out.

"Life was chaotic. Not at all 'standard.' This, though, gave me a different perspective on the world. I was eager to learn from others."

A care report, from when xe was 10, said xe wanted to get to university. Because no-one in xyr bio family had been. It was a struggle to get there. "So much to learn. But the cards you are dealt when you're born don't dictate the whole of your life."

Xe got into a grammar school – Handsworth Grammar. "There were," xe says, "plenty of 'Khan's'." That was likely uppermost in xyr mind when, at 18, xe opted for a complete change of name, a distancing from the family xe had left.

Although, xe adds, "I don't think my family background impacted on my identity. Rather, it affected my outlook. There was neglect and abuse. A lot else going on, besides. They always made me feel that I saw things differently. But I am neurodivergent. As an adult, in 2019, I was diagnosed with autism and adhd.

"Before that I had issues with social interaction. I have always struggled to maintain deep relationships. I did not want to restrict myself to one single friendship group. As a result, I am known for 'having fingers in many pies.' Deep friendships were not a big feature of growing up.

"Perhaps I was missing out. However, with everything else happening in my life, that was less important. The important thing was to survive. That led to me being homeless at times. Bottom line: both life experience and neurodivergence have had an effect."

One result has been that Adam is wary of any claim that there exists some absolute truth. "Truth is totally personal. It is relative to situation and person. For me, it is clear that societies and communities construct structures to fit their own needs and wants.

"It's a lot easier to see the world as relative from a

neurodivergent view."

Xe is also a member of Mensa. "I've been there since I was 11. I get that some people have issues with that. However, tests showed I am good at problem solving. I went through mental health services because I suffered from PTSD, anxiety. I was also diagnosed as bipolar. None of these were real barriers. But they were definitely a feature of where I was because of what I went through. At the same time, I had resilience and an end goal in mind. These helped me to go on."

Meanwhile, Adam's understanding of gender was growing. It was an evolutionary process. Driven, xe suggests, by learning more about xemself, and from the communities xe was involved in. In 2019, xe came out as non-binary. This followed xyr election as President of LGBTQIA+ society at Coventry University.

For xem, though, gender identity is fluid. The terminology xe uses reflects that. As it evolves, so will xe. In 2023 xe felt xe understood more about xyr gender, and started to also identify as agender. It fit!

Xe says: "I'm not opposed to having more layers to identity. I am relatively in the public eye. I don't feel I should hide." This, like xyr name change, is about self-assertion.

"There has been no major pushback directly. However, many people interpret my gender presentation as 'cisgender guy.' So, they feel it is OK to talk about trans and non-binary stuff in front of me. A lot of people end up saying they don't get it."

Although many don't notice, Adam has opted for some change of gender presentation. Xe has had laser hair removal.

Xe has changed xyr name. Also, socially transitioned. Xe bemoans the fact that legal recognition does not exist at all. Xe tells me: "I have applied for a world passport. Because it is a proper passport with markers that recognise non-binary status. The gender marker is an x."

Some battles, though, matter more. The biggest Issues, for xem, are erasure and lack of recognition. Government is binary. Banks are mostly binary. Xyr only option is to fall back on the 'umbrella.'

Non-binary and trans can be identities in themselves or umbrella terms. Adam's gender identity sits outside the male/female binary. In most cis-het circles xe will intro xemself as non-binary. Within the trans community xe will introduce xemself as agender.

Or as xe puts it: "My gender identity is... not gendered at all!"

Helen: Taking her time

Now 60, Helen came late to the transition party. Still, better late than never.

Ironically, she tells me, she knew she didn't fit her own skin; was aware of some sort of mismatch as early as 3 or 4.

"The first time I was able to describe who I was in a meaningful way was when I was 14. I came across Jan Morris' autobiography, *Conundrum*. Key passages from this have stayed with me all my life. For the first time, I realised that gender identity could be other than that assigned at birth That helped me to crystallise who I was in terms of gender. I saw myself.

At the same time, Jan went to great lengths to emphasise how difficult transition had been. "So, now I had a much clearer idea who I was. But I also felt there was no hope of doing anything about it. I needed independent financial means. This, back then, was as remote as the Moon.

"I tried to find out more. I drew a blank at my local library. University libraries were not much better. And TV in the 70s was very negative. Extreme caricatures. About the only thing that struck a chord was Hinge & Bracket. Very ordinary in appearance and demeanour. They showed it was possible to be trans and something other than caricature.

"Knowing this could never be, for me, was distressing. So, I avoided anything that hinted at gender transition. I pushed it out of my life. I compartmentalised to exclude all possibility of 'sex change.'

"I considered myself a straight male. I didn't have the vocabulary to talk about it. I had no role models. No information. The 70s was still the era of hard copy newsletters. It was hard to connect with peers.

"I went to a few meetings of gay soc at university. Some close friends were members. But it was entirely comprised of gay males. Perhaps somewhere with bars, night clubs, I would have had a better chance of exploring. As it was, nothing told me otherwise; that what I wanted was impossible.

"I set out to build a very male persona and career. The idea was to hide any possible ambiguity from others. I got into typically male activities. Then it was science at university. Nothing must betray the least clue. Though, do we do what we do because we enjoy it? Or do we enjoy it because we're doing it? How much of who we are is foisted on us?

"It was around this time that I met my partner. We married, in the 90s, and had two children together. Nothing rushed, though. That likely played a part in keeping us together later. My career was bubbling along slowly. Then, in the late 90s, along came the web.

"You can guess the sort of search I was drawn to. One key find was Andrea James' transition roadmap. It was very American in focus. Very prescriptive. Also, a lot of negativity. Perhaps because US employment protections were less extensive than in the UK.

"The roadmap told me you had to remain completely stealth until transition. Then you had to leave your job. Cut all ties. There was a huge emphasis on self-funding. I downloaded everything. Still, a similar guide for the UK was nowhere to be found.

"The urge to transition never went away. I knew now that it was possible. But without any source of UK information, I just carried on suppressing. I vowed to take this knowledge to my grave.

"Fast forward to the 2010s, when everything came to a head. Another thing that held me back was fear. Online, it seemed bitter divorce was inevitable. Break-up would be difficult. Our children would end up without one parent. Now, though, the children were grown up. Our youngest had now turned 18. So, change would be simpler, more straightforward.

"I was also starting to realise that a lot of online tropes online were out of date. As transition began to look less impossible, so, too were my attempts to bottle it up. It was starting to look inevitable.

"Things were becoming more problematic. I started to drink. Suicidal ideation was becoming stronger, more frequent. Though I never did anything to make it real. "(Disappointingly, many specialist clinicians failed to make this distinction, and I had to remind them of the distinctions between suicidal ideation, preparation for suicide, and attempts at suicide).

"I read a bit more. I found more recent works that were helpful. Optimistic, even. Virginia Erhardt's *Head over heels: Wives who stay with cross-dressers and transexuals*. Jennifer Boylan's autobiography, *She's not there*. It was not all bleak. A significant proportion of relationships survived. Over 25% of women stayed with their spouses.

"I also bought James Barrett's textbook, *Transsexual and other disorders of gender identity*. This had the advantage of being British and recent. It was also, at the time, the only one in the field. It was hugely useful as it highlighted what was current. Most important, it was clear that the outlook was no longer negative.

"I'd avoided contacting support groups, but I read forums. Now, I began to plan my transition timeline. I was ready to come out to my partner in 2017. Then, a major spanner in the works. My wife's father went into a final decline. I held off. Then held off again for some months after his death. It was very hard to do so.

"Then, 2018. My partner and I used to take long weekends away. We had a nice grown-up weekend booked, with self-catering, in Shrewsbury. We did the usual cultural stuff. But I had prepared a letter – a document – for her. This felt the right way to do it. It ensured I would say what needed to be said. All of the points, in the right order.

"On Saturday we had a meal. I felt like a condemned criminal and this was my last meal. I hoped we would stay together. I feared otherwise. The next morning, I handed the envelope to her. She sat. she read. Her first words, after, were: 'how long have you known?'

"Then, beyond all hope: 'I'm here for you.'

"It was totally unexpected. When I gave her the envelope, transition was the last thing on her mind. The only thing she could think of was divorce. So, my decades of disguise had succeeded.

"I felt – I feel –fortunate and privileged.

"We told our children the following weekend. They were fine. One even took the opportunity to come out as bi. Likewise, the wider family. Both sides. Friends, too. Though one or two did a double take.

"It was time. At that point, NHS Wales still required local mental health teams to vet individuals before putting them forward to the gender service."

It was a regressive system, and NHS Wales held on to it longer than the rest of the UK. Then, they changed, and overtook everyone else.

"At my GP's, I encountered my first hurdle. They were fine. Happy to send me to the local psych team for assessment before seeking the funds to send me to Charing Cross.

"The glitch?

"As always, the problem seems down to individuals within the NHS. Some are awful towards trans people. But, back then, I had no inkling how many GP's do not send referrals on. Or, talking to trans friends, how random is access to transition.

"In my case, it turns out someone in the practice did not pass any correspondence to my GP. Oversight? Or something else? I shall never know. Despite this, my experience was broadly positive. My assessment by the local mental health team was low-key. Not adversarial at all. The psych team supported referral. I waited another couple of months for the Welsh NHS to give the green light. Once I had that I transitioned in work.

"Within a month of coming out, I was living as myself at all times. Except at work. I'd delayed coming out there until I had a firm referral. When, finally, I did, HR was positive. Ditto managers. The head of HR said my approach was a template for the future. For example, one of the managers though it would be helpful to put out a press release out. I was encouraged when that was roundly rejected. But just having that exchange was useful learning.

"I put together a short email for all the staff. I met the team and explained. The Head of HR had already set out the position. So, there was no need to quote legislation at staff. I did a very short PowerPoint. Just six slides. Two or three people had trans people in their lives as family/friends. A load of my female colleagues gave me a hug. One male colleague did, too, adding 'I've got your back.'

"A few female colleagues quietly approached me to ask about hair and electrolysis. As my hair grew out, I wore a wig for a while. It all went well. But this is public sector and all the right policies were in place.

"Almost no-one has slipped up with pronouns or dead-naming. A couple of managers have difficulty, but it's not malicious. Part of my role is public-facing. So, I tend to be misgendered on the phone. Rarely face to face.

"I know this is partly 'passing/blending' privilege. I am also fortunate in being older. At a certain point, women – cis and trans alike – become invisible. From late middle age, one is much less seen. I used to encounter 'male gaze' more. But as I have aged, I, too, have become invisible. It is a godsend.

"I'm glad I'm not out on the club scene. I can see how many trans people are driven to withdraw from society.

"4 years from seeing my GP to referral to surgery. How lucky I was! When Wales upgraded its approach, everyone referred to the Tavistock was 'repatriated' to a brand-new Cardiff clinic, which opened in September 2019. Had I not been one of that cohort, I would only just be getting my first assessment now.

"Doubly lucky. Because online feedback and Welsh support groups suggested it was a lottery. Get the wrong psych, for your local mental health team assessment, and funding could be blocked.

"Still, I don't see it as fast; will never call it that. I first accessed HRT, in 2019, through a private provider. Back then, there were only four: Gender GP working online, YourGP in Edinburgh, the London Transgender Clinic, and GenderCare, also in London. I was able to explain that the last was not dissimilar to being referred by the gender service because it had the same clinicians and the same protocols. My GP was happy to go with a shared care arrangement. So, by the time I arrived at Cardiff, I already had 12 months of NHS HRT on record. They had no objections.

"Cardiff follows WPATH[13] protocols. That means only one psych opinion is needed. So, surgical approval was not long delayed. In fact, I got it at my first session. Three months later, I had my second surgical assessment. Also, by then, I was fully NHS. Surgery would have been 2021. Until Covid intervened. In the end, it was 2022.

"47 months from seeing my GP to completing medical transition! It could have been even quicker without the pandemic. NHS Wales moves faster than other trans healthcare providers in the UK.

"Still, I am not impressed. My story highlights how luck, privilege and knowing the system helps short circuit the bureaucracy. By the time I put in my application, I had immersed myself in the system and all the regs. I could quote them at whoever I was talking to. I read all I could about the impact of HRT. I knew what to ask for; when; who. This enabled fast

13 World Professional Association for Transgender Health

transition.

"Not everyone is so fortunate. The English gender service will get you to a first assessment quickly. But then there are long waits between appointments. Cardiff shows how transition can be made less onerous. NHS pilots have also helped.

"Still, it galls me that the process remains so much a postcode lottery. Not all my trans friends have been treated as well. Two had referrals to Charing Cross too early to get repatriated to Cardiff. So, they were referred before me. Yet they are still waiting years later to get surgery.

"That is why I now moderate on online forums. I want to help others by setting out a roadmap and guidance. My hope is that, in some small way I make transition easier for others.

"It's all about passing on information. A lot of the same questions keep coming up. So, I have built standardised answers/reference posts. It's a daunting process. But the trans community has always been thus; it has always supported its own.

"I support demedicalisation. Completely. Because the reality of psychiatric 'diagnosis' is that it is self-diagnosis. Psychs write down what you tell them. It's all about a trans person convincing a clinician that they are trans enough. Clinicians are still gatekeepers.

"The NHS Wales approach and the pilots are good. But they are not the real solution.

"In hindsight, I realise I should not have been so nervous. So tearful. Transition should be an unremarkable life change.

You shouldn't have to spend months, years summoning the courage to begin transition. Being gatekept, being asked the same questions at every single stage. I know that once I came out, I instantly felt much better about myself. There should be much less anxiety about coming out.

"The model needs to be one of informed consent. Because, if you are trans enough to have begun transition, you are obviously trans enough.

"I hope that one day, people are able to transition younger. Above all, I wish that transition will come to be seen as just one of the many potential life events people may experience. No big deal."

Jason: Winning family round

At 23, Jason is a determined young trans guy with his whole life ahead of him. But it wasn't always thus. There has been much grief along the way. Because when he needed it, his family was just not there for him.

When I spoke with him, he told me he always knew he was a boy. But for a long time, he'd never even heard the word 'trans.' He says: "It started when I was really young. I was saying stuff like 'I wish I was a boy' when I blew out the candles on my cake. In nursery, aged just 4, I asked another boy to explain how to wee standing.

"I always told people I was a boy. At 10, I started to put this into action. I played football. Loads of the other kids thought

I was a boy. No-one knew about me playing with my mates. At 12, I discovered 'trans.' I told my told mum, and her Initial reaction was weird. It was all downhill from there. The day I came out was football training day. After school I came home to her crying asking if I still wanted to play football.

"I expected some less than perfect reaction from my family. But nothing near as bad as it was. I think part of the reason people stressed out was religion.

"My dad compared it to terrorism. He said trans people were 'manipulated by the internet.' My sister was OK. But she always has been. She's a social worker with a good insight into different lives. Still, there was nothing she could do about it. My nan was upset, though I guess this was hardly surprising. A cousin came out as gay; has been with women ever since. Rather than acknowledge this, nan always talks about 'J's friend.'

"Grandad was the best. He was first to call me 'Jason.' Not out of understanding, but out of love. He could not be bothered to understand it. But nor was he bothered to make a fuss. Later, when I started my medical transition, he drove me to all my appointments.

"School was better than home. My teachers were good. To begin with, I was bullied by other pupils. Technically, I came out in year 7. But the year group already thought I was weird. I retaliated, making a video that took the mick out of the questions being asked. After that they were cool.

"The year group that came after were less good. Likewise, the year above. There was some support; but a lot of abuse.

Verbal. Physical. Other pupils - mostly boys – seemed to think they had a right to touch me. Changing rooms for PE were awful. Girls would stare constantly; mocking me. From that point on I was a "pervert." Especially when they found out I fancied a girl in my year.

"Because of how things were at home, I couldn't carry on living there comfortably. It felt like they were trying to bully the trans out of me. I was never kicked out. But I drifted. I stayed at my friend's house a lot of the time. Other times I'd just walk my dog for hours and hours. At night. By day. That was one well walked dog. Especially after I fell out with my friend over a silly argument.

"At 13, or thereabouts, I was still playing football! My mum wanted to look after me, but she was afraid of my dad. She wouldn't use 'Jason.' At least, though, I could talk with her, and confide. She also wanted to leave dad because she was sleeping with another guy. Though she redirected this by claiming it was all because of how dad was treating me. It was never properly resolved, and I – not my parents! – ended up in counselling.

"Mum is now much more accepting. In fact, all the family are great. What turned it round came about a year later. Mum and dad were back together. I was carrying on as normal, not showing depression or anxiety. Then it hit. I attempted suicide and at that point was diagnosed with gender dysphoria. 'Oh!' the family went. 'It's a real thing!' Not quite the words used. But that was the gist.

"After that, it was (relatively) plain sailing. Apart from the waiting times. I was in the system. They gave me an internal exam. Awful! Also, an MRI. I'm not really sure what they were looking for. Maybe they were checking for intersex features. I had psychoanalysis; got transferred to the Tavistock; and at 16 I got puberty blockers.

"I had no sense of being pushed down a pipeline. Though, I've not faced any real barriers. Well, apart from the waiting times.

"I had top surgery – a mastectomy – in 2022. Waking from that, the staff told me I was the happiest patient they'd had that day. I was just shaking hands with everybody! Also, the hungriest. I was first in line for surgery. Unfortunately, my GP had not sent bloods down. So, they had no idea what anaesthetic to use. I ended up at the end of queue. Only that meant starving *all* day. When I woke, they gave me fish, chips, and mushy peas. I hate mushy peas. At least, I used to. Now I love them.

"I am waiting for bottom surgery. Hysterectomy, and a phalloplasty. I've just had my second opinion, and at the end the psych went 'well done.' I'd be much happier if it was faster. Because delay is having bigger knock-on effects. But right now, it is about a 5-year wait. Going private is not an option, so I'm hoping for a cancellation.

"Bureaucracy is an issue, too. The doctor at the gender clinic said I should get it done through my GP. The GP says I probably can't get it (hysterectomy) done through NHS. Now the psych is saying I can get it done through the clinic. I want this done, because I don't want to be on hormone blockers forever. It's probably safe to stop now. But there is always a risk of periods re-starting.

"Despite that, I'd say I'm now mostly happy. I'm training for a career in zoo management, and studying under Chester University.

"Still, my life is made shit by the media. Too many people start arguments because of something they have seen on the news. A few years back, folks were fine with trans people. But the same people now want to argue. There are a lot of very ignorant people at university. As a result, I am increasingly forced to go stealth, because it feels like it is becoming dangerous to be out. I do not talk about it as much as I would like.

"I am sad, too, to lose friends for nothing I have done, and never know why. People who don't know me as trans share anti-trans comments with me. One day I will come out, and they will be surprised.

"Regrets? None. I just wish the world was a kinder place."

I exchanged the pain,
that I carried like a wait.
Unbearably long and sharp.

I took and gained though.
Some calm after the rain.
Sighs, smiles, I was brave.

But much more to give.
And take, of course, in return.
The hidden extras.

I gave up my ease,
with which I could breeze, around
folk, streets, minds and eyes.

I took feared worry.
Freezing solid with disdain.
A draining paining.

Paining for the ease.
Sighing smiling for the pain.
The counting is in.

Damned 'to do' or 'don't'.
Only now I am afloat.
Look, I am waving.

Barter, by Kacey de Groot

Transition delayed: a dark history

The dim and distant: trans past

I am no fan of raiding the history books for evidence of transness in some dim and distant past. Modern labels do not fit historic cultures well. That is as true of trans as it is of gay, feminist, or even 'man' and 'woman.' Individuals who might today be considered trans might, in other ages, have been labelled gay or effeminate. The boundaries of what was considered homosexual behaviour have shifted markedly over the centuries. Meanwhile, those claimed for modern feminism, or liberalism, often had values very much at odds with their modern versions.

Still, we have lately seen authors claiming that trans is some sort of modern fad. Unknown before the noughties, or 90's, or some arbitrary date. They should have done some actual research! For this reason, the corrective is important. Tales of individuals and groups that could have fitted within a modern definition of transness have been with us at least as long as recorded history.

One start point might be Roman Emperor Elagabalus. In the 3rd century AD, they were dressing in feminine manner, and demanding courtiers address them – her? – as 'Lady'. They may even have attempted some primitive form of surgery. Elagabalus, though, was beaten to the draw by the cult of

Cybele, which reached Rome almost half a millennium earlier. Cybele, the magna mater, was attended by priests assigned male at birth. These, 'Galli,' though, wore women's robes, and opted for castration. Were they trans? Perhaps.

I might remind you of the likes of Tiresias, or Hermaphroditus! Both mythical characters, who figured prominently in classical literature. Both heroes - or heroines - of some most eye-watering divinely inspired gender-bending. Yet, long before these, somewhere around 4000 BC, came Inanna, Sumerian goddess of love, war, and fertility, who also was believed to have the ability to change a person's gender. A millennium before Cybele, Inanna's worshippers were celebrating her power by transgressing the socially imposed gender binary of that age.

Post-Rome, evidence of cross-dressing and - more importantly - trans identity pops up with alarming regularity for anyone claiming the trans state is some sort of modern aberration. Famously in the 18th century, the trans baton was taken up by the Chevalier d'Éon. They claimed to have been assigned female at birth, but lived much of their adult life as a man. Transness also crops up in classic medical treatises. A state referred to as the "Scythian disease" gets regular mention. First, in works attributed to Hippocrates, who lived in the 5th century BC. Then, with increasing regularity in medical works from the 16th century onward.

All this, of course, relates only to transness as seen through the prism of Western culture. However, across the world, across time, there is ample evidence of cultures, from the

Indian sub-continent, from Indonesia, from North America, wherein a third gender was not merely permitted, but in many instances, considered superior. Possibly because individuals in this category might be considered to have a more complete knowledge of what it means to live in either gender.

None of this is intended as 'gospel.' The key take-out here is that there is good evidence that transness is not some modern mania. It has been around a very long time indeed.

The rot sets in: rise of the medical model

Early optimism...

Evidence for attitudes towards trans people suggests that until the late 18th century, most folks were minded to 'live and let live.' Yes, trans people were the butt of jokes; a suitable topic for parody. But there was no great drive, from officialdom, to dictate individuals' gender identity.

So how- why - have we gone from a position of relative tolerance to where we are today? Why are regimes across the world locking individuals up for the crime of being trans? I would volunteer two factors.

The rise and spread of an evangelising Christianity; and the creation of a normative scientific edifice. Central to both is a tendency toward judgment: dividing the world into right and proper ways to live, and wrong and improper. The former was loaded down with 'baggage' when it came to anything even remotely related to sex. It would be central to efforts to divert 'savages' away from their pagan, uncivilised ways, and convert them to right-thinking, God-fearing Christianity.

This received a boost in the form of an obsession on the part of 'soft sciences,' over finding universal and widely applicable 'rules.' Such rules were literally 'normative.' For they divided the world into right and wrong ways to live and to be.

Somewhere into this mix, one must throw an increasing enthusiasm for enforcing strict gender roles. In the workplace. In what one might wear. Sumptuary Laws, enacted by Henry VIII, and continued under Elizabeth I, set out strict penalties for dressing 'above one's class.' The 19th century ushered in an age of modesty, leading to a stricter policing of gender. Albeit that women who dressed improperly were more likely to be subject to social disapproval and public ridicule, rather than legal sanctions. It was also the era where gender segregation was codified into law in many parts of the US.

It is against this background that the first medical definition of 'trans' was coined. In 1886, Austrian sexologist, Richard von Krafft-Ebing described *'metamorphosis sexualis without paranoia*.' It was, he thought, an intersex condition. His influential book, *Psychopathia Sexualis,* provided a 'typical patient narrative.' That is, the patient history that forms diagnostic criteria. These, in turn, supported trans affirmative care for a generation of trans people. It also, of course, placed transness firmly within the sphere of medicine, with its implicit assumption that it might be viewed as dysfunction and, perhaps, 'cured.' The 19th century was not big on ideas such as natural variation, or diversity!

This breakthrough was assisted by early twentieth century advances in endocrinology. Across Europe, laboratories were experimenting with hormone replacement therapy. In the 1920s, trans woman Lili Elbe, better known to modern audiences as *The Danish Girl*, after the film of the same name, was transitioning. At the same time, a young aristocratic trans man, Ewan Forbes, was an early guinea pig for testosterone. Clinics in Austria, Germany, Hungary, Czechoslovakia, and Paris supported transition. So, Ewan– and other early trans pioneers –travelled widely in search of medical intervention.

The very first gender identity clinic (GIC) opened in 1919 in Berlin. This was Magnús Hirschfeld's Institute of Sexual Sciences. It provided affirmative healthcare, including reconstructive surgery, to trans men and women. But Hirschfeld's Institute was short-lived. On 6 May, 1933 the Nazis destroyed it. They burned its books, and sent its patients to death camps.

It would be thirty years before another attempt was made to centralise medical services for trans people. For the next few decades, it was a question of seeking out the few clinicians who would provide affirmative care. In the UK, this meant endocrinologist Joseph Adler and surgeon Lennox Broster. Both were based at Charing Cross Hospital in London. Also important was the work of innovative plastic surgeon Sir Harold Gillies at Basingstoke. Or you could pay one of the so-called 'Westendocrinologists.' Specialists practising largely out of Harley Street. Being trans was still seen as an intersex condition. So, UK trans people were able to self-identify, receive affirmative medical care, correct their birth certificates, and live in complete equality.

Into the wilderness

This began to change in the 1950s. In her important book *How Sex Changed,* Joanne Meyerowitz describes the outright hostility that US trans people faced from psychiatrists. Ranged against these were endocrinologists, such as Harry Benjamin, who offered a supportive care pathway. He had worked closely with Magnus Hirschfeld; and he treated Christine Jorgensen, widely recognised as America's first trans celebrity. The high profile accorded her case led scores of trans people to seek treatment with him. But publicity is a double-edged sword. Publicity around Christine's case, as well as that of Roberta Cowell in the UK, stirred up abusive press coverage. Transition should have been a private medical matter. Instead, it was turned into a heated public debate. A focus for cultural insecurity.

One anxious response was a new medical theory: gender identity. In April 1954, an acrimonious debate broke out on both sides of the Atlantic. The opening shots in a turf war between psychiatry and endocrinology. It was fought out mostly in the pages of the *British Medical Journal* and the *American Journal of*

Psychotherapy. The prize? Trans healthcare. But Benjamin and Gillies were in their seventies. Broster was about to retire. They had little appetite for confrontation. So, psychiatry won the day.

US psychologist John Money pushed the theory that children are born with a 'gender gate.' Appropriate parenting would enable them to pass through correctly, avoiding the twin evils of 'gay' and 'trans.' If a child *were* gay, or trans, then it was the parents' fault. But never fear! Psychiatry could cure them. Well, it could try.

For some strange reason, many anti-trans writers cite Money as a moving force behind the advancement of trans treatment. Whereas little could be further from the truth. As far as trans people are concerned, he will always beknown for the outrageous treatment of David Reimer[14]. The latter was born a "biological male." However, he suffered irreparable damage to his penis as an infant. What to do? Simple. Money decided to impose transition on him, by means of a forced and non-consensual gender reassignment. In modern parlance, through assault and child abuse dressed up as corrective surgery.

Despite the unethical nature of his approach, Money built a career on the back of it. He published widely; and his 'research' was instrumental in encouraging widespread surgical intervention for intersex children.

It was not until he was 15 that Reimer finally learnt what had

---

14 Gaetano, P. (2017). *David Reimer and John Money Gender Reassignment Controversy: The John/Joan Case | the Embryo Project Encyclopedia.* [online] Asu.edu. Available at: https://embryo.asu.edu/pages/david-reimer-and-john-money-gender-reassignment-controversy-johnjoan-case.

been done to him. However, he had suffered severe gender dysphoria for years previously. He rejected the female identity assigned to him, and began living as a male. Despite this, he suffered a lifetime of severe depression. In 2004, aged just 38, Reimer took his own life.

Meanwhile, in 1962, the first Gender Identity Research Clinic opened at the University of California, Los Angeles. Its aim was to 'cure' gay men, lesbians, trans, and bi people. Aversion techniques, ECT, psychotherapy, and frontal lobotomy were its chosen tools. In other words, a patient pathway that began with conversion practices. Just 30 years on from Hirschfeld's clinic, which celebrated and supported trans people, UCLA scare-mongered and suppressed. Its model was quickly followed by New York and Toronto.

Trans people whose 'delusion' persisted might be mollified with HRT. Those who were persistent, insistent, and consistent in their 'florid psychosis' might be given reconstructive surgery. But only if they 'passed' extremely well. Good news if you were a trans woman of slighter build, and had good cheekbones. Not so good if you were tall, had larger hands or a disinclination to adapt to 'proper' ladylike habits.

If you wish to understand the resentment felt by many trans people when dealing with gender services, it starts here. For this was all about psychs telling trans people who they could be. What they could be. Even, whether they could be considered trans at all. Based on little more than a set of dogmatic prejudices based on next to no research whatsoever.

The irony, of course, is that many of the most prominent proclaimers of this new scientific orthodoxy – Freud, Jung, etc., let alone Money and his disciples – were in no acceptable sense 'scientists.' Their 'expertise,' from 'Oedipus complex' to 'penis envy' was a construct created out of middle-aged male navel-gazing. Little more than charlatanry, infiltrated into modern parlance by constant repetition. Yet, through a process of attrition, it is their views on transness that have dominated mainstream discourse.

The fall of the NHS

In 1969, John Money and psychiatrist Richard Green imported this model to the UK and the NHS. The First International Symposium on Gender Identity was held at London's Piccadilly Hotel. Shortly after, the NHS set up a new centralised service at Charing Cross Hospital. This was presided over by psychiatrist John Randell.

His role, as he himself put it[15], was 'to breed out of our genetic inheritance those with psychopathic and adverse genetic propensities.' Or, if that is not clear enough: 'some form of eugenics, in fact.' This take has been given a new lease of life in the 2020s, as some gender critical 'feminists' have argued openly that it would be better for all if there were just⊠ fewer

15 John Randell, *Sexual Variations* (London: Priory Press, 1973) p. 146. [online] Cited by Zoë Playdon in https://transactual.org.uk/blog/2022/03/16/gender-identity-clinics-genesis-and-unoriginal-sin/

trans people.

Patients were coerced into believing they were mentally ill. They were groomed into compliance with the GIC's demands; blackmailed by reminders of their psychiatrist's control over their future; and required to 'consent' to sterilisation.

This non-consensual, no-choice regime was supported by the publishing of one legal decision, and the hiding of a second. Both dealt with privilege. Both reflected establishment fears that wider acceptance of transness could upset the apple cart when it came to passing on property and titles.

The one published was a ruling in *Corbett v Corbett*, a divorce case heard between November and December 1969. Some years before, Arthur Corbett (later Baron Rowallan) married April Ashley. He knew she was registered male at birth. He knew she had had gender affirmative surgery. When the relationship broke down, Corbett looked to end the marriage. His legal argument? The marriage was invalid from the outset. Because Ashley was 'of the male sex.' The judge agreed.

In effect, he declared April and all other trans people to be mentally ill. Frauds. Trans people's civil liberties were removed. Without parliamentary debate. Without statute. Trans voices were erased by media lampoon and attack. It is distressing to acknowledge that these three conditions - legal exclusion, biological elimination, and cultural obliteration - meet the formal criteria of genocide. What the Nazis could not achieve in the 30s, the UK would attempt again in the 60s.

This decision contradicts precedent in an earlier case. In

1952, Sir Ewan Forbes corrected his birth certificate in order to marry. This was quite routine for trans people then (though a bit more complicated in Scotland than England). His male status was later challenged by a cis cousin, over the inheritance of a baronetcy. But, in 1968, little more than a year before the Corbett case, the courts found in favour of Ewan.

Academic and author Zoë Playdon has investigated this case in depth. In *The Hidden Case of Ewan Forbes*[16], she argues "there is apparently no reason why the benefits [this case] provides should not be enjoyed by everyone else in the UK who like him has been born with the condition of transsexualism."

Yet that case was not available to the court in the second case. It was 'hidden.' Ironic. Or perhaps not. His legal win was seen as so threatening that the media was gagged. Those involved were sworn to secrecy. All records of it were concealed for decades.

In this darkest period of trans history, trans people had few alternatives. Money gave you access to private healthcare abroad. Or through Harley Street. Or through those few isolated practitioners still offering affirmative care. New support groups were set up. The Transsexual Action Group [TAG]. The Transsexual Action Organisation [TAO]. The Self-Help Association for Transsexuals [SHAFT]. These grew up to provide community help and to share experience. They taught

16 Playdon, Z. (2022). *Hidden Case of Ewan Forbes: the transgender trial that threatened to upend the british establishment.* [online] London: Bloomsbury Publishing. Available at: https://www.bloomsbury.com/uk/hidden-case-of-ewan-forbes-9781526645876/.

others how to survive the GIC system. They also signposted the most helpful (least abusive) medical care available. Following the Stonewall riots in the United States, there were stirrings, too, on the political front.

Socially, however, trans people had been stripped of all rights. They could no longer correct birth certificates. That meant they had no proof of identity for employers and officials. Their private medical history was on display any time they applied for a job with a pension, or health insurance. It was legal to fire someone on the spot for being trans. Legal to send trans people to the wrong prison. You could refuse any and every kind of service, affiliation, or entry to trans people. Even more sinister, driving licences were secretly coded. So, police and others 'in the know' would be aware they were dealing with a trans person.

Meanwhile, the medical establishment consolidated its position. The International Symposium on Gender Identity continued meeting. In 1977, it persuaded the World Health Organisation to adopt its definition. Trans was now 'sexual deviation centred around fixed beliefs that the overt bodily sex is wrong.'[17]In 1979 it reorganised into the Harry Benjamin International Gender Dysphoria Association. This agreed a set of *Standards of Care* intended to protect its members from 'legal, ethical, or moral scrutiny and liability.'[18] In 1980, 'transsexualism'

17 World Health Organisation, *International Classification of Diseases* 1: 1 (Geneva: WHO, 1977), p. 197. [online] Cited in https://transactual.org.uk/blog/2022/03/16/gender-identity-clinics-genesis-and-unoriginal-sin/

18 Coleman, E. (2009). Toward Version 7 of the World Professional Association for Transgender Health's Standards of Care. *International Journal of Transgenderism*, 11(1), pp.1–7. doi:https://doi.org/10.1080/15532730902799912. [online] Cited in https://

was added to the American Psychiatric Association's *Diagnostic and Statistical Manual of Mental Disorders* [DSM-III].

GICs now had absolute control of trans people's lives. This was deployed pretty much at the whim of individual psychiatrists. Some believed being trans arose from childhood psychodynamics. Others thought it represented aberrant behavioural imprinting. For Freudians, it was all about 'guilty sexuality.'

Despite their claims to expertise, Gender Identity was not a clinical specialty in the UK. There was no agreed terminology. No diagnostic criteria. No care pathways. No clinical standards, outcome measures or regulatory frameworks.

Or as Dr John Dean put it in evidence to the Women and Equalities Committee in 2015, on the origins of gender identity clinics: "there is quite considerable diversity of opinion between different clinicians and different clinics. All seven gender clinics in England arose out of the special interest of an individual a long time in the past. There has not been a lot of planning of their development, and there certainly is no training pathway for medical practitioners or others who work in this field."[19]

GICs could – and did - do as they pleased with helpless patients. We have no idea how many trans people failed to survive this regime. For they were not part of the UK's public

---

transactual.org.uk/blog/2022/03/16/gender-identity-clinics-genesis-and-unoriginal-sin/

19 John Dean, 'Oral Evidence: Transgender Equality Inquiry,' HC 390, Tuesday 8 September 2015. London: House of Commons, p. 9. [online] Cited in https://transactual.org.uk/blog/2022/03/16/gender-identity-clinics-genesis-and-unoriginal-sin/

health record.

The first glimmerings of change came in 1996. A legal victory in the European Court of Justice in 1996 restored employment rights. Trans community groups focussing on legal and administrative change made rapid progress. In 2002, the UK government stated formally that being trans 'is not a mental illness'.[20]

However, the supposedly 'game-changing' 2004 Gender Recognition Act [GRA] was a setback. Parliamentary debate made clear: sterilisation was a general expectation for granting trans people some limited civil liberties. In addition, the GRA set up an anonymous medico-legal panel to decide on applications. Without meeting applicants.

Far from improving the lot of trans people, the process reinforced GICs' unaccountability and incoherence. It further embedded the NHS-wide mistreatment of trans people, recorded in 2013 by thousands of tweets on #TransDocFail – a spontaneous community scream of outrage at how individuals had been treated on a day-to-day basis by medical professionals.

20 Department for Constitutional Affairs, *Government Policy Concerning Transsexual People*, July 2002. Now archived at https://web.archive.org/web/20080511211217/http://www.dca.gov.uk/constitution/transsex/policy.htm. [online] Cited in https://transactual.org.uk/blog/2022/03/16/gender-identity-clinics-genesis-and-unoriginal-sin/

one foot in and one foot out
hopping back and forth between
your world, my world, the one we could make together
the one you can't talk about,
the one you convinced me I don't want,
my chest heavier with each step, each step longer,
time under the knife
stacked with the bodies you're hiding
footprints running through realities,
realities running away
truth obfuscated, I fawn for you
moments passing through, around,
up or down and never in between
and everything,
everywhere, all at once, or twice
and having fingers in many pies is delicious
or it would be if I could taste the jam
on my hands
but it looks like blood sometimes
and, you know,
I'm allergic to raspberries anyway

parallel universe, by Zee Y

Transition Stories: II

Jean: Going Dutch

Trans folk sacrifice much to transition. But sun, sea, and scuba diving in the Caribbean? Who would do such a thing?

Well, Jean, for one. Jean is 23, and from the Netherlands. She was born down south, near the borders with Germany and Belgium. But, she owns, "I definitely had a silver spoon. Not set up for life. But not badly off, either. A few years back, my grandma left a house to the family. So, we moved to the coast: a small, picturesque municipality in the north."

Since then, she has lived in the Amsterdam area, only moving back to the countryside during Covid. Later this year, she is off to university in Leiden. There she will begin research for her master's in archaeology. Although "Much of the uni is very much old guard. Conservative. So, I am slightly anxious."

Her passion is Caribbean archaeology. "I stumbled into this. The earliest residents arrived in Curaçao[21] in 3000BCE. When Europeans arrived, there were already a fair few indigenous people on the island. Most were deported as labour by the Spanish. The Dutch continued this process. Those living there were taken to mainland Venezuela. In their place, many more African slaves were brought in.

Now, though, living in Curacao, pursuing a passion for

21 A small island country in the Caribbean, formerly a Dutch colony.

archaeology… Perfect? Not for Jean. "From an early age I had a sense of 'girlhood.' I started having issues in early puberty. When I was about 12. I was not at all comfortable in my body. Or with masculinity in general. I was forced into sports and in early teen years my body consciousness became more intense.

"Life sucked. Increasingly, I felt that if I'd been born a girl – or turned into a girl – all my problems would be solved. But I grew up in very heteronormative/cisnormative groups. If you ask a young person what a binder or HRT is, I doubt they'd know. I had a better idea of trans people as a result of my own feelings.

"I knew that trans people existed from high school. But it was all very general. It also framed trans people very much as some 'other.' It was always framed as 'some people can have these feelings.' And 'some people born as a boy want to be girls, and vice-versa.' Never 'You could have these feelings, too.' So, I could never connect what I felt to 'feeling trans.'

"However, my feelings did take me to less cisnormative communities. So, I guess I was better informed than most.

"But through my teen years I insisted – to myself – that I was not trans. So, I kept moving the goalposts. Get good grades in school. Get a girlfriend. Life will fix itself!

"I was less focused on body parts. In my 20's, I became friends with girls. Especially lesbian girls. But I wasn't enjoying life. I could not love, and be loved, as I should. At best, I would disassociate. At other times, I found myself tipping into depression.

"So, I ran away from who I was. All the way to the Caribbean.

I think I had this quaint idea of starting afresh. In January 2022, aged just 21, I crossed the Atlantic to do a scuba diver instructor's course in Curaçao. I was there for 6 months. Finally, though, I knew. Denial wasn't working, and I could run no more. I was trans. Worse, scuba diving forces you to confront your body every single day. My world crumbled.

"In June, I called my GP in the Netherlands to request a tetanus shot. I also told them: 'I have been suffering from gender dysphoria for long time.'

"I didn't know how this would go. Netherlands is still quite conservative. Trans people remain mostly invisible and at the sharp end of (institutional) transphobia. Even ten years ago, sterilisation was mandatory if you wanted to 'change sex.' It's not as bad as the UK. All the same, it could be better. It can be three to four years' wait for a first appointment.

"I know I am privileged. Just a couple of weeks to see my GP. Then I signed on to the waiting list for a number of clinics. Seeing where the waiting list is shortest. I signed to a psych clinic that specialised in gender dysphoria. They then assign you to a medical clinic. In January 2023, I had my first appointment and over the next three or four months I got a diagnosis. After that I worked through the process with them. Making sure there was nothing else that might get in the way. For instance, they check whether an individual has decided to freeze their gametes.

"This took me to September 2023. By then I had already started self-medding. Technically illegally! I imported HRT from a source in Turkey. The meds I ordered were the same as on my prescription now: Cyproterone acetate and a6mg oestrogen supplement. But they cost more. Also, they can be impounded if you're unlucky. I got my baseline blood values. I've also had a more recent test, because my 'endo' requested it.

"And I am having an argument with an insurance company about lasering. A specialist has been brought in to see if there might be an issue with passing. This, in turn, impacts whether my insurers will pay for facial feminisation. I will likely get that done privately.

"Over the last few months, I've started opening up to friends one at a time. They've been fine; have reacted positively. As a result, I am now truly a part of a group of girls. They just opened their arms and invited me in. They help me with all kinds of stuff, give advice, invite me to events, pull me out of my shell a little. It's really great!

"My family knows, now, too. They are putting pressure on me to tell more. The first person I told was my mum, who has aways been very supportive. She has even bought me some clothes! Dad is more sceptical. He's not outright anti. But he does not understand, and it has created a sort of wedge between us. Brothers are good

"Curaçao is off the cards for the immediate future. I can hide changes to my body. For now. Also, longer term, I will pass better by starting young. However, dysphoria and 'the trans angle' are much less accepted in the Caribbean. Returning, I would run a much greater risk of bad things happening.

"Starting to transition, I feel like my life has had a number of resets, because I have had to try out many things. Now, I know, I have a long road ahead. Finally, though, I have a sense that there is track in front of me."

Nur: A new beginning

For Nur, coming to the UK has been a mixed blessing. Now 31, he has lived in London since he was 23. He arrived here from Faro, in Portugal, around 8 years ago. Since then, he/they has been working in a hospital as an occupational therapist. Though, when we spoke, he was just about to start a new job.

Mixed. Because, as a trans guy, the UK has welcomed him. It has allowed him to start his transition. But it has not been entirely positive.

I ask: when did you know you were trans? "That," he responds, "is a tricky question. Because there were times I did not want to know. I preferred to hide the truth even from myself. I'm pretty sure I knew as a child. Because I was very angry at everyone wanting to put me in a group of girls. Only, I felt I did not belong there at all. I remember being very angry, too, when mum tried to put me into something more girly. One time, I told her 'I am not a girl.' I must have been 8 or 9.

"I definitely repressed it as puberty came on. Any time I said I did not want to be a girl I was met with laughter. Or shame. Even if I just tried to be a tomboy. Mum would make fun. It was pretty obvious that life was harder if you did not conform.

Of course, Portugal is Catholic; and Catholicism and culture blend. So, values are very traditional. Family plays a big part in everyone's life. It's getting better now. But difference is very much frowned on. It's still OK to be homophobic. As for being trans! That's just odd.

"I went to school. I got older. I didn't have many friends. I suppressed my feelings until I 'became a girl.' Because I was ashamed. Because I needed to keep up appearances for my family. I was about 15 or 16.

"Fast forward, and moving to London was a breath of fresh air. It put some distance between me and my life in Portugal. It allowed me to make a break with my family. Still, it took me a long time to let go. I went into therapy because I was unhappy. Something wasn't working, and I felt stuck. I didn't know what I was looking for. But it helped. It gave me the freedom to think. Then 3, 4 years back, I started seriously questioning my gender. I went through a stage of thinking I was non-binary. Now I consider myself a trans man.

"From there it was a short step to starting to transition. Within the UK. I got a referral to gender services in 2021. I knew there was an enormous backlog. So, for a while, I was resigned to that. Then I did more research and realised I could start hormones privately. I contacted the London Gender Clinic. There were some issues with my bloods. But, once those were resolved, I started taking testosterone in May 2023. As for surgery, I'm taking my first steps to go through top surgery.

"It's now been nearly a year. I wish it worked faster. I'm

already starting to see some changes, and that feels incredible. I feel like I'm not lying any more. People get to see me for how I see myself. There is one change, though, that is still in the pipeline. I haven't changed my name yet. Because in Portugal you have to apply to a court to do that. My name now is short for my legal (female) name. But I will be changing it.

"I've had incredible support from my friends and from my partner. Though, I do re-assure her that I will not be a 'manly man.' That support has helped me get through the process with less fear. I can be confident that there is help and support there if I need it.

"Telling family was much harder. They've still not got to grips with me being gay or queer. I told them 10 years ago, and they're still trying to catch up. I knew I could not just sit down and tell them. Instead, I wrote them a letter. In it, I told them I was trans; that I was going to start to transition.

"My sister acknowledged the letter. She told me she understands and supports. My parents have said nothing. Since then, my mum has asked a couple of questions. But I don't think she understands very well what transition is. The problem is, I always struggled to discuss stuff with her. Our relationship has never been good. Shortly after I began hormones, she asked me if I was going to have a beard. She asked 'why are you doing this? You can be with your partner without having to transition.'

"I wasn't close to family in the first place. We still have regular communication. Transition, though, is an unspoken subject, even though it's happening in front of their eyes. I go back regularly. But that causes more problems. They still use my dead name. My old (female) pronouns. When I went over at Christmas, other relatives could see my face and voice have changed. As topic of discussion, though, it remains taboo.

"There are only a couple of friends I'm still in touch with in Portugal. An ex-girlfriend. Another from high school. Both have been very supportive. Likewise, people in London. Work have been good, too. But the NHS is fairly inclusive.

"All the same, attitudes more generally have definitely got worse over the last five years.

"I've started having some negative experiences. My gender is increasingly ambiguous. Somewhere 'in the middle.' People keep trying to figure me out. Over the last couple of months, I've had far more people staring at me on the tube, on the street, in pubs. They're trying to figure out my anatomy. Utterly shameless. I've had a few unpleasant situations, which I did not expect. I expected people being curious. Not aggressive. Not scary.

"Last week I went to a pub outside London. I went up to the bar and when I sat down, there was a man looking at me and staring. He kept staring. I got up to go to the loo. I wasn't sure which to go into because of all the staring. So, I went into the ladies. When I came out the man followed me to my seat. I sat down. He asked me my name. Such entitlement! He wanted to know who I was. What was my gender.

"That is the scariest it's been so far.

"Now that I'm transitioning, I feel better. At the outset, I didn't know how I'd react to being correctly gendered, which is happening more and more often. That's had a huge impact. Because it turns out it is an immense relief. My dysphoria is, like, 100 times better. I'm constantly taking pictures, comparing differences in my body.

"Transition has changed how I see myself. It has changed my life already. For the better."

Michael: DIY and just living their life

Michael is great. A young trans guy, born in Amsterdam, but British. Living now in leafy Sussex, which is also where he did most of his growing up. Pretty much always in the middle of nowhere. "I've never lived in a village," he tells me. The first inklings he had of being 'trans' came up online, when he was about 14. "In Sex ed," he explains, "they hardly mention it. They never tell you stuff properly. So, I had no idea. I didn't even know that trans was a thing. It makes sense now. Then, though it felt like the biggest tragedy of my life.

"Before then, at 10 or 11, I had a sense that something had gone wrong. It started with me feeling very disconnected from my body and what was going on with it. I felt separate from everyone else. Socially, I was an anxious child. I've never been very comfortable with people generally. So, never a massive tomboy. This was more something not quite right about myself and the people around and how I related to them. That feeling went into overdrive at puberty. And wow!

"There wasn't an instant rejection of femme stuff. I was out of sorts and funny about the feel of clothes. I'd wear long skirts because they were comfy and I liked the colours. It wasn't 'I am not a girl; I shouldn't wear that.' Only, as I got older, I began to feel more pressure to gender conform.

"At 14, I did not talk to my teachers. There was no communication. No connection. I didn't tell my mum, either. Though, I did ask if I could get my hair cut, as it was very long and I wanted it gone. I was getting desperate for change and a space to figure stuff out.

"Eventually, I made an aborted attempt at coming out. Initially as non-binary, as that felt like a useful stepping stone. I told my mum and she was, like, 'what is going on?' I think she was confused, taken aback and just a bit frightened. So, she shut the conversation down. But she did her best to encourage me to keep talking with her.

That first coming out gave me more time to think about gender. So, I was better prepared when I came out the second time, a few months later. As a trans man. In the summer of 2019, I came out to her for the final time. I waited - kept it to myself for a while – because my parents had separated. Slowly I told friends and other people, until, by the end of the year, everyone knew.

"In the interim, she had time to think about what I had said, and come to terms. Before I came out properly, I asked if ever she ever wished I'd been born a boy. She dismissed this out of hand. Now, she'd had time to process. So, when I did come out properly, she was ready and accepting and lovely about it. Still, it took her a while to come to terms with changes to my name and pronouns. There was some grief, too, over taking down of photos in the house. But she is a single parent, and I think she managed very well.

"My younger sister really struggled to begin with. She was 7, and she was worried: 'Oh my god, my older sister is disappearing'. She's not transphobic. She just could not get her head around what was happening. Now, she's over it and very good. So much so, she corrects other people on my behalf.

"I've also tried to engage with NHS gender services. I've been on a waiting list since 2019. I knew it was a long list, so when I was 16, I went to my GP and got a referral to the Tavistock. They have been in touch just twice. First, to check if I still wanted to be on the list; then, again, when I turned 18 to tell me I had two months to tell them if I wanted to be put on the adult list. So, I've accessed care privately: HRT through gender GP. And top surgery through another provider. Initially, my GP refused to take over the prescription. Because I was under 18. I went back again after I turned 18 and the GP still said they were not sure!

"I will keep applying pressure. They have agreed to do blood tests. But want to be arm's length. I suspect my current GP has never dealt with a trans patient before. Their predecessor, who has retired, would likely have done shared care. The current ones refuse. The nurses are wonderful. Unfortunately, doctors seem too scared to get involved. I need to bully them every step of the way, because their view seems to be if they can ignore me, they will.

"Now I get testosterone, but no anti-oestrogen. Gel, because I hate the idea of injections." (Author's note: I am so with you on this!). "Also, injections mean a much more uneven set of mood swings. It arrives monthly, by post, because Boots refuses to do HRT from gender GP. So, I have to involve a further pharmacy. It doesn't stop me; just makes life more complicated.

"I do not want any more surgeries. I am happy with how my body is now. But then, I never had massive bottom dysphoria. I absolutely wanted top surgery and HRT. I'm not so bothered by the rest. Is my body at war with itself? I think that's not so much the case for trans men.

"I do still get the occasional period. Some people stop. Others do not. I've learnt to become comfortable with them.

"I've been lucky. Hassle has mostly been to do with medical care. Friends are generally fine. Apart from one. She said 'fine.' Then she spent the next two years mis-gendering me and making inappropriate jokes. That's just casual transphobia and total disregard for my feelings. No-one has turned out gender crit. Though, a few people at school have been a bit shit. But mostly, they're positive. My grandparents have been a bit slow to catch on. I think they're confused. My grandma still asks if I'm a waitress. It's not my job and it would be the wrong word even if it was.

"I've not had major issues with loos. But there have been some pointed looks. In one pub I had a miserable experience when I went into the men's. People pointing to the sign on bathroom door. The problem is, some people identify me as female. Yet I also pass enough that I don't feel safe in the women's, either.

"Except, passing depends on what I'm wearing and how I'm feeling. I dress how I want to, pretty much, and sometimes, I dress androgynous. That can mean I pass a bit less in some instances. Too, some folks think I am a trans woman.

"Even if feeling safer in women's, would feel bad about passing too well and making people uncomfortable.

"Bottom line: I am not going to go in and pass as some sort of straight guy. I'm just not masc enough for that. I'm also not straight! So, there is a lot of confusion from people who do not know what is going on.

"It also can cause issues when people try too hard to 'get it right.' For instance, on an arts course, I had a mix of people addressing me as 'they/them,' while others went with 'he/him.' At least it wasn't 'she/her.'

"For all that, I am happy. I am good with friends and family; and I have confronted my gender issues early. Now, I just need to get on with the rest of my life."

Dorian: living his best life

At 26, Dorian is doing his best to deal with the slings and arrows of... outrageous gender services. He wishes things were better. In the meantime, however, he is putting his energies to good use by setting up and running a journal project called Transmuted. Or as the website has it, a "trans cultural project hell-bent on elevating gender non-normative discourse."

When did Dorian first realise they had issues with their gender? He – for Dorian is trans masc non-binary – says he has no idea. "I never fitted in to all the girly stereotypes. But that is true of many girls. It did not strike me as out of the ordinary, so I thought nothing more of it. I cosplayed my first day at college as a boy. I really enjoyed doing that, even though I did not know trans was a thing.

"I was past 18 when I went to my GP and said: 'I think I am trans'. At that point, I was studying at university in Reading. I must have been about 20. I didn't know much about the system. But I knew I needed a referral. They seemed to be OK about it. They filled out the referral and said they would send off.

"Later, I went back and they said the Doctor just never sent it off. It was not even on my record! Unfortunate accident? I wouldn't be surprised if this was a deliberate attempt to stop me from transitioning.

"It took me the best part of another year – a very bad year in my life – before I got an appointment with a gender clinic. But I never went, because of everything happening in my life at that point. So, by the time Covid came round, I decided I could not wait any longer. I had enough money at that point to start spending on a monthly testosterone prescription, and I went to gender GP. Then after two months, that changed and I did not have the money any more. It was all too stressful."

For now, work on transition is on the back burner. Dorian explains: "I've always been me. But my relationship with being trans is complicated.

"I can't just retract what I am; who I am. For now, though, I have decided I can cope with life as long as I never think about gender stuff. I've spent a lot of time looking at how privilege works in respect of gender, and I know that has influenced my need for transition. Yes, I want top surgery. Yes, I want testosterone. However, I am also very aware that that want is manipulated by how cisnormative society runs; how it dictates your experiences. So, I have learnt to cope.

"I can get away with not caring about how I look right now and not caring about wanting to look good. Instead, my focus is on knowing what is important. That means uplifting friends, comrades; and in that context, my body does not matter.

"Bottom line: I am still the person I would be if was physically transitioned. I am sure this Is in part a trauma response to not having control over my body in my earlier life. It represents, too, a fear of personal change. I have created a safe zone that is very important to me and the effects of transition seem a little too much for now. Though I am also very lucky in that the impact of HRT to date has not resulted in hair loss.

"It is complicated by the fact I am back living with parents. North of York; almost north York moors. My family is far from posh. Mum's husband is a farmer, and mum was happy to marry into that lifestyle. Otherwise, though, they are just ordinary parents.

"There has been parental pushback. My dad never believed me when I said I was trans. Though he thought it amusing to ask 'can I watch' when, a few years back, I said I was lesbian. Despite that, he seems to recognises who I am more than my mum has. She just decided I was 'confused.' Then she stopped talking about it.

"7 years down the line, she has begun to use my real name and pronouns, and now goes on about how great she is with trans people. She has absolutely no idea what being trans is; or about how little support there is for people with dysphoria. She refuses to accompany me into the men's section of stores.

"For a while I worked as a carer. Now, however, I am putting a lot more energy into my community. That, in turn, has led to Transmuted, a broad umbrella for supporting trans artists and scholars. There is a website[22], where we publish a lot of creative writing by our supporters. We also publish a journal, which we release intermittently, according to workload, and funds available!

"On top of that, we also host a number of events each year, both in-person and virtually. These include workshops that allow for community education, knowledge-sharing and open discussion. We also hold mini-festivals, which celebrate and showcase trans poetry, live music, drag, and other types of performance.

"I try to support that by putting a lot of work into social

22 Transmuted (2024). *Poetry.* [online] Transmuted. Available at: https://www.transmuted.co.uk/poetry.

media. I have also just set up a Community Interest Company (CIC) and I am going to start applying for grants. It's nowhere near enough to live off. There is no room for trans-specific pubs in most bookshops.

Still, it feels the right thing to do for now."

Gabby: In limbo in Ireland

If you thought transitioning was difficult in the UK, you should try Ireland. Gabby, 26, is a trans woman. Half English, on her father's side. But she's lived in Ireland her whole life. A small town in the midlands. Rural.

Now 26, she is a programmer with a degree in software engineering. She's hoping to get accepted for a master's course later this year. She is also moving forward with her transition. But the road has not been easy. Not least because, as she puts it, "the last couple of years of my life have been a blur. Much of my time was taken up being a carer for my grandmother. I was very busy; very preoccupied with her illness."

What about gender? "I never felt like a boy. Though the first time I talked about my feelings I was 6 or 7, and I did not have the language. I said 'I wish I was a girl.' Parents told me not to be so silly.

"We didn't speak about it for another 10 years. In school we 'covered LGBT.' Sex ed was mostly about gay and bi, and how people had to fight for their rights. I watched propaganda from the 60s and 70s, and studied that. They told me the T stood for transexual. We also learnt a bit about sexual health. Little more. We never talked about gender dysphoria.

"At 16 I came across the term for the first time. as soon as read about it, I knew that was me. When I started to tell them I thought I was trans they were not exactly surprised. Because since 11 onward, close friends knew that I hated being 'born male'. Now, though, I started to put a name to this feeling, and to think about medical intervention for the first time. But I was too scared to tell my parents or ask for help with transition. I'm not too sure what I was afraid of. It wasn't about physical stuff. I trusted that my parents would be accepting.

"But I'd seen trans people used as the butt of jokes in sitcoms. It felt like there was great stigma around it. That it was something shameful. So, not telling had a lot to do with internalised transphobia from portrayals I had seen. I also remembered my father making a transphobic 'joke' about the Wachowskis. 'I'll have to start calling them it.' At least my mum told him off for that.

"I was 18 when I plucked up the courage to tell them. They didn't take it well. They were very against transitioning. My father said I was lucky he didn't beat me. Because 'other fathers would have beat their son for saying that.' He thought I might have Asperger's, or be mildly autistic and insisted I get checked for that before I spoke to any professionals about gender.

"I saw a psych; told him that my sense of dysphoria was significant enough that I had been suicidal a few years previous.

In his letter back he diagnosed Aspergers; also noted gender dysphoria; and that was it. Parents were now happy for me to attend therapy for gender dysphoria.

"My options, though, were very limited. My GP said the only place they knew of was somewhere in Dublin. They had therapists and were partnered to a France-based psych, who took on many Irish patients because of the lack of support in Ireland.

"At that point, I still didn't know what I wanted. Medical intervention? Yes. But I was scared. I saw my therapist for counselling, but I was not actively seeking HRT at that time. Together, we began to explore social transition: clothes, change of name, in the privacy of own room. I was buying dresses and skirts online and it made me happy.

"Yet again, friends were OK; but I had to find the courage to ask parents how they would feel if I dressed that way around the house. They did not take well to that. Mum said if she saw me that way, she would not be able to hold a conversation with me. Basically, 'you can wear what you like as long as no-one sees you.' Her experience of men dressing in female clothing was exclusively from drag comedy, and men cross-dressing to make fun of women. When she did see me dressed, she was surprised that I opted for toned down simple dark colours.

"When she said no, I felt guilty again. Like, it must be something I am doing wrong. I kept on with the therapist for a while, but mum's comments halted any further progress. I was stuck. Also, the secrecy made it worse. At about this time, my therapist shut up shop, as Dublin hospital opened a service to treat trans adults (18 or over). I went on their waiting list while I was in college. Over a year to first being seen, though it's got worse since. I had graduated by the time of my first appointment; and by then, my mental health was poor. I wasn't really able to look for work, so I was stuck at home.

"The National Gender Service (NGS) told me I could have no medical intervention until I was presenting as female full time. They gave no time scale. Just that I had to be out publicly and living full time as a woman before they would provide any testosterone blockers.

"That was bad news given my parents' attitude. They came with me to one appointment; went along with pretty much everything the psych suggested. 'If that is what you have to do, that is what we will do,' they said. Then, the first thing they said in the car was 'you're not allowed to do it.' I was 22.

"The excuses kept coming. 'Grandmother would not be able to take it' - even though she had always been the most supportive. Then dad said I could not transition until he told his own dad. I was beginning to get angry at myself and my parents. Because, by now, I was sure I wanted to transition. I wanted HRT; wanted to live publicly as me. But everything was a flat 'No!'

"My mental health problems got worse. I think this was the first my parents understood how serious things were. I had a breakdown. In the shower. I just started screaming and crying. That seemed to terrify mum, and she was a bit more understanding of the pressure I was under. Even so, she sent me off to a local therapist, first, because she saw this as an emergency. No names, but that therapist later became infamous for their gender critical views. They were civil but tried to talk me out of transitioning or looking for medical intervention.

"Luckily, I dodged that bullet. Because she was also my mum's therapist, and seeing me could be considered a conflict of interest.

"So, it was back to another therapist in Dublin, and on to anti-depressants. My GP also prescribed SSRI's, which helped a lot with my anxiety. This kept me clear-headed. I was still with the NGS therapist and a local therapist, and eventually my mum said OK: I could dress feminine around the house. Not long after, they were OK with me coming out publicly. I also changed my name. 23.

"Puberty was definitely the worst point in my life. Because, then the dysphoria was at its height. However, public coming out was second worst. I did not pass at all. So, I got verbal abuse on the street. The first time out in public someone called me a freak to my face. Not a great start.

"Yet NGS were waiting for me to come out publicly before they would start evaluating me for t-blockers. I rang and told them I was out. The psychologist said they would see about setting up an appointment with an endo at the next visit. They never got back, and it was over a year before I got any kind of response.

"Every few months I rang for updates. I'd ask to speak to

someone on the phone: the lead psychiatrist took calls one hour every week, on a Tuesday morning. But I never got through.

"They said he would get back. Nothing. This went on for 15 months. I was still getting verbal abuse on the street. I had no idea why they were not getting back. Eventually the GP rang and introduced a new psych I'd not seen before. Turns out there was a note on my file saying I shouldn't be seen. Why? The Psych just shrugged. 'Maybe something Covid related.' I think it was incompetence and a mistake with paperwork.

"An awful appointment followed. I thought I would be seeing a psych and an endo. That was what they implied on the phone. I got a psych on his own, and he was thoroughly unprofessional. I wore a t-shirt and ankle length skirt to my appointment. He told me he could not imagine me in a dress. I was stunned, because this was the closest I could get to a dress without actually wearing one. I laugh now. At the time, I was very upset.

"I told him about abuse; the absent endo. I said it was making me feel suicidal. His response? 'If you mention that again, the session is over.' I was crying. I no longer knew what to do. I gave up trying to argue my case; just said whatever I felt would appease.

"They referred me to an occupational therapist. An endo was out of the question, because I 'had no occupation.' When I challenged him, he was evasive. It was, he said 'for all the points we discussed today.' One thing he asked me about was whether I was working, or in college. I said it was a bad time to look for work, because of the pandemic. His comeback: 'that's one of the reasons.' But he did not elaborate.

"At the time I did not read him as anti-trans. I was so confused. Since then, it has dawned that a lot of the people in the NGS are just hostile to trans people in general. Did I mention that the first time I saw the NGS, it was a three-hour session where they demanded my entire life story? Loads of invasive questions, like: what porn did I watch; and what genres was I specifically into?

"Since then, I have met people there who seem to want to help. But the psychs are actively hostile. After that appointment, I was devastated. I decided the system was not going to help. So, I would get hormones on my own. I contacted gender GP. They interviewed me over zoom. I told them I wanted a t-blocker and oestrogel as, throughout all this, I had been doing some research. So, I knew exactly what I wanted.

"They set me up with a prescription. Within three weeks of making contact, I took my first hormones. I could not believe it. Because I was now 25, and I had spent the last 7 years trying to access support through the Irish system. How could it be so easy, when people inside the system made it so impossible?

"It also highlighted the mental health catch 22. HRT was very like starting anti-depressants. My mental health improved, pretty much overnight, even though physical changes minimal. Since then, I've stayed better. I didn't tell the NGS that I had started HRT. But when they saw such a huge improvement, they were finally happy for me to go ahead!

"Also, my endo has been very good. They are one of the few people in the service who has been helpful and seems to care.

They are very transparent and let me see results of blood work so I can be involved."

It is about here that I paused the narrative. It's a sensitive subject, but Gabby has early onset hair loss. She started losing her hair when she was 20. So, now she is looking at getting a transplant. Except, this is something that could have been fixed. Or at least put on pause. And, once on HRT, likely reversed to some extent.

It's an issue for many trans women, and a source of extreme grief to some. So, I asked: did any of these highly paid experts, supposed specialists in trans healthcare, ever mention it? "No. Never."

I am raging!

Meanwhile, Gabby's parents had mostly come round. Though there were still some tensions. "I told my mum that giving puberty blockers to trans kids is essential to stop them going through the wrong puberty. That is what made me suicidal; and now I have to spend money on surgery to put things right. I'd have asked for them when I was a child if I knew they existed. My mum has seen how much I suffered. But she still reckons nothing should be offered until 18. Likewise, my father.

"My grandmother was supportive throughout. The best of all of them. I did mention I was her full-time carer for the last few years of life. I think that helped NGS' decision to take over from gender GP.

"But transition was not entirely alien to her. Because at one point, her brother had expressed trans desires. Though this took place decades ago, and in the end, he was forced to give up.

"Regrets? Only that I wish I could have started sooner. If only been I'd been let through the system sooner... Or, if only I had lost hope in the system sooner; gone self-med sooner. I've since given advice to people about going to the NGS. I tell them: 'don't expect them to help. You are much better off going elsewhere.' I have no faith in the system as it is."

Still, the future looks brighter. "I've started getting into freelance writing, I talk to others, which helps me feel better. I am passing on what I know to those who come after."

Ash: Beating the transphobes

Ash is 27 now. However, like many trans people before, he owns to having known something was up from a young age – perhaps 6 or 7. But he did not know what. Still, that is when he started asking about gender and how he was different from his brothers.

Why? He doesn't remember. "I just remember asking questions. But nothing really broke through until puberty hit. Then I realised two things. I was attracted to women, not men. And I had strong sense that I should have been born a man. It helped that my parents were never strict about gender roles. For instance, my brothers were allowed dolls."

School didn't really say anything about trans. "The main thing I remember about sex ed is having to put a condom on a banana! We all had to sign some paper saying we won't be homophobic if gay and lesbian things come up. Otherwise, they would explain stuff 'only if anyone asks questions.' Sort of, if you don't ask, they won't tell!

"At 19 I went to college in Northampton, my home town, to do a health studies course. There I joined an LGBT group and, for the first time, I met trans people. There were quite a few trans men and women in the group. It clicked. Before, I identified as lesbian and interested in women. Though I was never really femme; always seen as a tomboy. Besides, I'd long suspected I wasn't a lesbian. The label never quite fit.

"Whereas, now, I had a place that felt right. I did not have to be a certain way. I felt comfortable enough, safe enough to explore gender some more. First stop, I came out as non-binary. I just name changed amongst friends in college. Then, I followed up more formally in 2017: a deed poll; and a referral to a gender clinic.

"At 21, I went on to Wolverhampton Uni. Health studies again, with modules on biological health, mental health, gender and sex. It was a good broad grounding that opened the way to a range of careers.

"It was also about now I asked my GP to refer me to a gender clinic. They did. So, 3 years later I am just starting with Nottingham GIC. I asked to be referred there, instead of my closest GIC, as, at the time, Nottingham had a good reputation with non-binary folks!

"Though I had already started transitioning. In my first year at Uni, in early 2018, the Uni GP referred me to a "specialist endo clinic" in Harrogate, where I saw Dr Hammond. He's NHS, and used to be the lead endo at Leeds GIC. He did a basic assessment for dysphoria. I told him I wanted HRT; explained my expectations around hormones. He gave me an informed consent bridging prescription. So, at least I was not totally dependent on the GIC process.

"I came out to my parents before I went to Uni. That is, I left a letter behind for my mum to read. They have always been supportive and that continued now. Although, mum struggled a bit. She wasn't unsupportive. She just knew how bad being trans could be from a hate perspective. She worried I would not be able to cope with stigma and discrimination. Dad was fine. His first response: 'I'm glad I didn't get that tattoo with your names on.'

"Both my brothers accept my decision. Nothing much has changed.

"Nottingham GIC were supposed to take over my HRT and update my prescription. Unfortunately, during Covid, I moved back in with my parents and the online system failed. I sent emails and phoned a few times in between, trying to communicate change of address details. But they did not log that I'd changed address and GP. So, I didn't get the letter for some of my key follow-up appointments.

"It took a serious setback for the system to respond. In October 2023, there was a shortage of the HRT I was taking. I had to come off it. Only, after three months without HRT, I was feeling low and suicidal. I went to my GP; asked him if he could contact the GIC directly to change my HRT. Oh. Now they realised my details had fallen between the cracks! At least, they did write to acknowledge that.

There was then a follow up appointment with the nurse. In April 2024!

"Transition has not been entirely free of trauma. I've tried to just get on with it. But there have been issues with GP's throughout. Mostly, when I have sought mental health support, and they've brushed me aside 'because you're trans.' This, in turn, led directly to psychosis, and a stay in hospital in 2020.

"I am diagnosed as bipolar, so I take mood stabilisers. I'd started taking anti-depressants when I was about 17 or 18 and they did not help at all. When I went to college, I started on a different anti-depressant and the dose was increased. Until I ended up in hospital.

"That, in turn, led to consequences on the personal front. I don't date at the moment. It's not that I don't want to. I just don't know how. I dated when I was in in college and at uni. But don't really know when to tell someone I'm trans. I also had a bad break-up, following my admission to hospital with psychosis. It wasn't the only reason. But it didn't help. I was with a trans woman, during Covid. After lockdown, she was struggling with anxiety and going out as herself. In the end, I think it was just too difficult – for both of us – to carry on.

"Something similar happened in January 2023, when there was a shortage of my hormones.

"How so? Because, when I went to my GP to discuss HRT, he put me on an anti-depressant. For some reason he had no access to my records. He then decided I was making up stuff about being bipolar. In part, I am sure, this was down to anti-trans sentiment on his part. So, he pushed the antidepressant at the same time as my HRT re-started.

"For the next three months, I kept telling him about symptoms I was having. But he refused to believe me. Meanwhile, others I was speaking to could not tell me if it was the HRT or medication that was causing issues. Turns out, it was side effects from the drug – sertraline - the GP pushed onto me that was the problem! But the GP blamed the hormones, and wanted to increase the dosage of sertraline.

"I went to A and E. I had an emergency appointment with the mental health team. They took me off medication. Everything was sorted. My HRT was changed back to where it should be. Unfortunately, there were other difficulties. Once again, the result of cis folks not getting how trans healthcare works.

"Because my HRT used to be by injection, and every four weeks. That leads to t-levels going up and down, with a massive spike once a month. Now I've switched to a three months prolonged release. But it took six weeks to get my hormones levelled off. During that period, I did not have support from the mental health team. Should I have? I certainly expected more.

"So that's the down side. Not dating. Currently unemployed. But I've worked in healthcare for the last 7 years. Perhaps less out than I could be. Because transphobia. And I am looking to do a master's in psychology.

"I don't want top surgery. In fact, right now, I don't want any surgery. I'm a bearded young man; and I have got to where I want to be. Mostly winning. Life will sort itself out."

Andie: From stealth to self

Oh dear. Meeting Andie for the first time, I feel just that bit 'seen.' For Andie is a trans woman who was born, like me, in the late 50s. She, too, came late to transition, and for reasons that are not all that different. Now she gives of her time supporting others in the community. Answering questions. Providing a little stability in a world that seems at times to be utterly out of kilter.

She tells me "I knew next to nothing of anything LGBTQ before I was 13. My parents came from a traditional religious background, and alternated evangelical with more liberal beliefs. It wasn't exactly a subject for discussion. It was a given that I would attend church regularly.

"I didn't exactly hate my body. I just had little idea what to do with it. From around 5 or 6, I felt more comfortable with girls. Not as a boy 'hunting' them. That felt so uncomfortable. But as one of them. For a long time, my best friend was a girl. I was also very happy not 'doing boy things' – I guess I simply didn't understand boys.

"I still remember a thing that happened when I was in the fourth year at junior school. We had a great teacher. One of the good guys; a bit alternative. We also had separate 'girls' tables' and 'boys' tables.' One day, though, this teacher said we could move around to where we liked. I went and sat on one of the girls' tables and it felt amazing. Being with the girls. No longer surrounded by boys. It was so right.

"So much of what I did was about being more like the girls. Which may be why I had no real male friends before I went to (boys) grammar school. It felt safe. Much safer than being among male friends. I committed very strongly to my girlfriends; hung out with their (girl) friends. I felt very left out when events were girls only.

"I always had an aversion to male clothing. When I was about 8, my mother tried to make me wear what she called my 'little man's overcoat'. I loathed that coat; not least because it was making me a 'little man.' (Later, my wife would want me to wear an overcoat, be the smart mature man; again, I hated it as much as the really short hair I felt obliged to have.)

"By the time I hit puberty, I'd say I was uncomfortable. Confused. I spent pocket money on girls' underwear, that I would wear secretly.

"How do you live with that? For a while, in the 60s and 70s, hippy dress codes offered some relief in colour, style and the unconventional. A sense of freedom. At some point in secondary school a girl in my class invited me out to church. For a few years, I went very evangelical. Hardly surprising, given my earlier upbringing. It gave a belonging but also a tremendous sense of guilt, and a profound fear of being found out.

"It was highly prescriptive, and came with a very particular view of sex. Set out what you could say, think, do. Anything LGBTQ – or any sex outside marriage – was deeply sinful. I was trapped. The topic was taboo at home, I had no diverse friends, I had gone to a boys' grammar school; and, a little later, we were into Section 28.

"All I knew about trans was that it was 'deviant.' A perversion! I was consumed by guilt, guilt, guilt⊠ Fear and loathing and no way to escape from myself. Of course, I froze out any possibility that I could be 'transsexual.' It was unthinkable.

"Ironically, the girl who introduced me to that church went on to have a lesbian relationship at university; it ended our engagement. She never knew about me.

"I married at 25 – after a third engagement. My vicar expressed concern at this. He'd picked up on how I was a serial committed monogamist! My first relationship lasted 4 years. Then a German girl, for 2 years. Then another for 2 years before meeting my wife of 30 years. I always had to be with a girl to be comfortable. A series of intense relationships without a break.

"Still, in 1982, the woman I married knew a little about my cross-dressing. I'd been scared to death of being found out; tried to keep stuff hidden, supressed. So, I was OK to find a minimum level of acceptance. But it wasn't fully real. She saw it as an acceptable sexy secret. She did not know about my discomfort at being male. She got that I was different from other men, knew I was uncomfortable with 'manliness.' Not the wider stuff.

"For a long while, it worked. I was (mostly) happy in work. I enjoyed my career; a succession of jobs in publishing, info tech for libraries, and a long time in social research. Then, more recently, author, editor, illustrator for technical guides. I was happy, too, to be a parent. I had two children: a son, and a daughter. Though I really hated any 'dad' jokes. The stereotyping and the assumptions. Over time, my secrets become ever more burdensome. The thought of discovery was a nightmare. I felt like I had to be 2 people at once – and one of those a complete stranger to me.

"For a long time, I wished I *could* be discovered. Then I wouldn't have to pretend. What broke it for me was finding an early text-based social media site called the Experience Project. People created groups around interests. Others joined. Discussion followed. I realised there were whole communities out there who were trans, and this helped me start to work out who I was; who I wanted to be. I got to know some people on the trans forum very well. They provided me with a new perspective.

"I discovered that being trans was an actual, natural thing. I realised I was trans. It came with an overwhelming sense of relief, excitement, dread. Also, an urgency to be known. Because 'OMG. This is real and feels so right. Why could I not have known earlier?' Also, 'How do I convey this feeling so it will be understood?'

"Then, 2010. I was made redundant in November. That gave me space, time, and enough funds to take a breather and see what happens. One of the first things I did – in secret – was visit a wig shop. Then I went and bought some new clothes. With the wig fitted I ended up looking like my sister.

"Wow! Can I really look like this? In spring 2011 I joined the Clare Project group[23] in Brighton. I realised soon enough that I had a decision to make. My wife was working four days a week. Son was away at uni. Daughter was working two part-time jobs. With so much freedom at home, I started building a secret double life. It felt wrong. I tried not to be dishonest. Slowly I leaked my truth.

"At Easter 2012, I announced to every band and group in which I was playing trumpet, that I was returning after the break as a woman. No issues. I guess this was the beginning of my 'social transition.'

"In terms of wider family, my son was fine. He had a trans friend at school, so this was less of a shock. My daughter was not accepting, and I have had no contact since.

"Both my mother and my sister were supportive. In 2013 we even went out as three women, together. Wider still, my nephews and nieces are OK. My cousin is not. Definitely anti-trans.

"Sadly, my marriage did not survive the upheaval. We had couples' counselling. My sense, though, is my wife never intended anything other than to give me a soft landing. She gave me an ultimatum after she discovered I had been to a GIC and had a psych assessment: 'if you go further, it isn't with me.'

"I had no choice but to walk away. I could not bear living with and loving someone who no longer loved me. I asked her

23 The Clare Project provides a variety of support options for the trans, non-binary, and intersex (TNBI) community in Brighton and across Sussex. https://clareproject.org.uk/about-us/

to divorce me, because I didn't want to invent the required blame for an 'at fault' divorce, and wanted a gender recognition certificate as soon as possible. In 2012, we separated. We sold the house; got divorced. We're no longer really in touch; but it's not antagonistic.

"On my own, I started getting used to being different. There was celebration in it. Freedom. Every day as my female self was a huge release. Though it was tainted by a sense of being regarded by some as perverse. Resentment, too, at everything holding me back.

"Also, loss. Grief and deep disappointment that I had to cut myself off from all I knew. That being authentic meant being rejected; and that I had only been wanted for what I was not. I dipped into suicidal ideation just the once, though, when I felt that I could 'never be either a woman or man' and therefore never be accepted socially.

"On the other hand, I had the support of (new) friends. There was daylight ahead.

"Then it was 'into the system.' Through the gender clinic evaluations with a goal. Real engagement, with an end in view.

"I spent the next two years being looked after by Charing Cross GIC. Hope, and frustration!

"It was all very ordinary. I turned up in a dress, and played it as straight as I could. I explained I'd been living as a woman for a year already; asked why they were asking if I was committed. I also let them know I'd started HRT in 2010. Via the Internet. Their response: 'Yeah, most people do.'

"2013 was excruciating. I was frustrated, angry, impatient. My body was developing and changing. My dysphoria was getting worse, the more incongruent I became. Nothing could happen fast enough. I knew what I wanted. So, why weren't the gender service actually helping?

"I was not going through this lightly. I was deeply self-analytical and understood that while this was a decision, it was not a choice. No-one was persuading me. This was just something I had to do to live with myself for the rest of my life.

"Why can GICs not communicate? Why are appointments always so far away? How hard is it to prove who and what I am? What was not 'real life experience' about what I was doing? At one point there was a year wait to my next appointment. By then I had been socially transitioned for two years. Finally, I was recommended for surgery and the funding had been approved – but it had never been communicated back to anyone.

"It was sheer fluke – only by talking to a friend who knew their way round the system – that I found out. So, summer 2014, I achieved my goal: surgery and completion. Two years from start to finish. Not bad. But I snuck in as one of the very last to pass into a functioning system. I had friends, only months behind me, who missed that boat. They were then delayed a further year or two years. For me, though, 2014 was a big year. The triple: surgery, divorce and GRC!

"Hospital was a matter of fact, welcome process. A happy and fulfilling time for me. I woke from surgery with a sense of tremendous relief. I could go forward, and leave "the system" behind forever. Now I could be myself, be ordinary, get on with life. Not be gate-kept or controlled, judged, evaluated, waiting for permission. Careful, but not stealth. Anyone can find out about me if they really want to.

"It's not been all plain sailing, though. I didn't get much system support. I was never offered voice therapy, or hair removal. Nothing that might have made transition or 'RLE' any easier or more affordable. I had to ask for everything. Endocrinology was superficial at best – never saw an endocrinologist – and my GP didn't have much clue. They did eventually arrange annual blood tests.

"In 2019, I had a deep vein thrombosis. Their only suggestion was that it was caused by the HRT. Maybe it was, maybe it wasn't.

"My workplace was not terribly well-versed in handling a transition, or safeguarding employee privacy. But I learnt to be assertive, and I survived. In my current workplace, no-one much knows or cares about my past. Now locally, at work, socially, I am just a very ordinary and authentic me. That makes me happy.

"Never for one moment have I hesitated, regretted, or wished differently about any decision or course of action I have taken since I realised that being trans is real and is OK. In fact, I shudder to think about the alternative. Would I be dead? Unable to live a life of hating myself?

"In 2014, I found a new (cis female) partner: someone who is comfortable with who I am. We are still together, and own our own home. At first, I was optimistic about improving trans lives and recognition. Less so since, as gender critical voices have gathered and gained political influence, especially from 2019 in opposition to GRA amendments. GC views, groups and individuals do impact me. But avoiding them means losing social involvements I used to have.

"These are hurtful times. Dangerous times. We are all affected; all that much more guarded.

"I am grateful now to be helping others, as chair of trustees of the Claire project. Earlier this year, I marked my first day of semi-retirement. I am glad that things worked out. Very glad, in the end, to be able to say, openly: 'I am who I am'."

Phoenix: Born again non-binary

If you're non-binary, finding a place to 'fit in' can be complicated. At 21, though, Phoenix reckons they have started to find some answers. Right now, they are at university. Studying psychology. Their focus is on clinical and health psychology and everything to do with mental illnesses.

They tell me that their sense of being non-binary came from when they were very young. They did not fit with either gender, but... "I did not have the language to explain it. When I hit my teens, my first thought was this was just the stereotypical body hatred that many report in the face of change. Then I found there were words to explain what I was feeling. Dysphoria. Also, it was then that I started to discover non-binary people and understand what it means in practice.

For me, being non-binary means living as a human, not a gendered being. I wear the clothes I want, not because gender tells me to wear them. I want to be treated as a person above everything else. I want to be treated like a human being.

It is linked to feminism. Because gender is so inherently linked to language, you are talked to differently. The words used; phrases, terms. There is also a lot of fuzziness within the trans community. No-one can really answer the question 'what is this gender?'

In daily life it is mostly about pronouns. Also, other things that people avoid around me. Like, 'not ladylike' or 'too masculine.' It means moving through life in a non-gendered way. I get the definition of agender. Though personally I don't use it.

I realised I could accept myself as non-binary, and everything just seemed to fall into place.

I told my family about 2 and a half years ago. Dad took it well. He went out, and did some research. He talked to HR at work; asked them for advice as to how he could help me. Mum did not take so well to it. She is very transphobic. Her view is that people are groomed to be trans. She is pretty much a cliché white conservative, who watches the mainstream news. She doesn't do anything to stop me directly. She just rants at me; and I tune her out.

That's why I waited til I went to uni before telling her. I knew, if I told her when we were living under the same roof, it would not end well. I knew that she would go on and on about 'being groomed.' She has since tried to stop me seeing my friends. Because, according to her, they 'made her (sic) trans.' So, by stopping me from seeing them, I might come back to my senses.

I changed name. Dad was cool. Mum was upset. She constantly deadnamed me. My response was to be very strict, aggressive, any time she did that deliberately. So, that stopped. Now, she avoids using my name altogether. I am 'the youngest one.' Which is technically correct.

I am the youngest of three. I have two older brothers, who reacted well. Both wanted to know why I wanted top surgery. I wanted it in order to get away from a more gendered look. They listened to what I had to say. Both very accepting.

Mum realised she could do nothing to stop me. Instead, she kept trying to persuade me not to go ahead.

I knew I would have to wait forever within the NHS. So, I started raising money to go private. On campus, I did this through regular bake sales. Mainly cup-cakes. Usually plain vanilla. I did cookies one time. Also, a SpongeBob SquarePants cake. But cupcakes were easiest. Self-contained, and no messy cutting. I'd take any donation. £1. £10. Once someone gave me £50!

They were a great experience. Loads of people came up and were nice, supportive. A lot of trans people stopped by and told me 'I thought I was the only one.' There was no pushback on campus. Though I was a target for some of the usual student bad behaviour. Some people came up, a load of guys, plus a couple of women. They milled around laughing and saying that

I was raising money for HRT for a trans woman. Then one of them claimed they had given me some money that they meant to donate to a bake sale set up beside me. In the end, they stole £10. As they left, I could hear them laughing about 'a trans woman.'

I set up a GoFundMe; got a summer job, too. Because top surgery is not cheap. It's now just over £9,000. And it's done! In August, just gone.

Right now, I do not want HRT. I prefer staying androgynous. Besides, being on HRT is expensive, if it's not funded by the NHS. I could try for a bridging prescription; but I'm not optimistic. My partner is trans. They've been on the phone asking for a blood test but the GP said no. They used a loophole to get out of providing one as the blood test wouldn't be done due to her presenting with symptoms to the doctor. Rather, because she is about to start medication.

Under the NHS guidelines it is therefore up to the GP to decide whether to run the blood test and he denied it to her. Even though he knows how dangerous it is to not check hormone levels before going on HRT. Luckily, I managed to do another bake sale and sold some old clothes online, and I managed to find a private blood test online. This was not easy to do and I did not eat well that month. Luckily, she has now managed to start HRT and is loving her results!

"Regrets? No. None. Everything has worked out. I'd have loved it if my parents had helped with the surgery. In the end, they did not.

"Other than that, I am very much of the view that society needs to stop making laws about non-binary people without involving non-binary people.

"Nothing about us without us!"

How can I write you a love sonnet
When language is so gendered
Are you both my king and queen
Or something in-between
Love knows no bounds so why
Should it fit so neatly into their binary
And how can I live in a world
Where the love of my life
Is not recognised
And so I must fight with you
Against this culture and to
Wards a path where
Genderless souls and
Genderless love
Are free

How can I write you a love sonnet?, by Anon

Things can only get better?

A century ago, trans people self-identified. We received affirmative medical care from endocrinology and surgery. We corrected our birth certificates and lived equally. From 1970 onwards, UK GICs removed autonomy, curtailed consent, and played a leading part in trans genocide.

At the same time, they feigned innocence. They posed as caring supporters of trans people. Psychiatry dominated the GICs. Trans people, with no confidence in the good intentions of the clinicians, coached one another on how to survive it. Community forums were rife with advice on how to get to the endocrinologists and surgeons whose skills they needed. It was a system degrading to patients and the NHS alike, and long overdue for change.

For a while, things did begin to get better. Then they got worse again. Much worse.

Theory vs practice

It begins with a vast and growing gulf between theory and practice. In theory, trans people have the right to medical treatment. This is supported by law, ever since 1999, when the High Court ruled that North West Lancashire Health Authority were wrong to impose a blanket ban on providing gender re-assignment surgery for three trans women. This ruling was upheld on appeal.

The problem, though, is a very English one, albeit delivered somewhat in the style of Irish cleric and philosopher Bishop Berkeley. He was much concerned with the question of whether reality could be said to exist separate from our perception of that reality. "What happens if a tree falls in a forest, but there is no-one there to hear it?" You may remember him from Philosophy 101.

Like so many other well-loved quotes, it seems the good bishop never actually said it. Still, the underlying message is clear. If a thing 'happens' and there is no-one around to bear witness to that thing, did it really happen?

Or, in the case of UK-wide gender identity services, you have a right to receive treatment as a trans person. But does that right truly exist if your first appointment lies 5, 7, 10 years in the future? [24] Or if health practitioners and others charged with delivering those services opt out? Or place obstacles in the way of those seeking treatment on 'individual ethical grounds'?

As of April 2024, TransActual reports, wait times for first appointments at gender clinics range from 1 to 8 years. In most cases, add a year - or more - before an individual is likely to be allowed hormones/HRT. Then, several years more before any surgery. In the case of trans masc surgeries latest figures

---

24 Sadly, the answer, according to UK courts, at least, appears to be a resounding yes. In January 2023, the High Court rejected a challenge by the Good Law Project in respect of the long waiting times experienced by trans people seeking help from the NHS. The court held that NHS England was doing 'all it reasonably can' to reduce waiting times. This verdict was upheld following an Appeal in August 2023. https://goodlawproject.org/update/good-law-project-will-appeal-high-court-decision-on-trans-waiting-times/

suggest you need to add an extra five years.

Moreover, these waiting time estimates are historic. That is, they are based on someone being seen for a first appointment today. Forecast wait times – those for someone being referred today – are significantly longer.

Even this, though, may be over-optimistic. For there is evidence that some clinics are massaging figures down by keeping a second list. A waiting list for those waiting to go on the official waiting list.

Why? The most obvious reasons are Covid hangover, and a generally failing NHS. This, in turn, is driven by austerity, under-funding, and generally appalling industrial relations. All are true. All have affected pretty much every aspect of the NHS in the last few years. But waiting times were always bad.

When I first decided to transition, I approached my GP. Could he refer me to the Gender Service, as then was? 'Happy to,' he replied. Still, I should know it was likely 18 months wait for a first appointment. Outrageous! In the end, thanks to cancellation, the delay was more like 9 months. The appointment, though, was one of the single worst hours that I have ever endured. 60minutes of insult and hostility, starting with a near refusal to use my chosen name. It ended with me in tears and suicidal. Which is not at all me. Well, tears yes, as anyone who has ever sat through Les Misérables with me will confirm. But suicide? Never. Until I engaged with Charing Cross.

Once bitten, twice shy. I never went back; never engaged with them again. As 'luck' would have it, my mother had passed on a few years previous. A bittersweet kind of luck. For it meant I could afford to be treated privately. But I was never able to come out to her. Never able, perhaps, to obtain her blessing.

As for Charing Cross, no doubt I now figure somewhere in their stats for desistance. Or not serious about transitioning. The reality: I was done, dusted, and post-op many months before they got back to offer a second insult. Or appointment. Again, in my old name. Also, to grovel. Because they never noted my new name. So, they had no idea where in the NHS to send the bill for the session I had already had.

Earlier, I mentioned my sadness at the detransition of one young trans woman, who lived locally. In 2022, four years after applying to the gender service, she heard back. A letter informed her that they had not even looked at her application yet. But they hoped to look at it with a view to inviting her to a first appointment at some point in the next year or so. That's 'look at it within the next year or so.' Not at all the same thing as a date for an appointment.

Reports from across Europe highlight just how grim the UK picture is. Transition begun and in many cases (surgically) completed in significantly less time than it takes for the UK gender services even to get back to a trans applicant.

This is compounded by the fact that there is no great rush to specialise in gender identity services. In the previous section, we took a brief tour through the gatekeepers at the heart of the UK gender identity service. The system puts them in positions of power, entitled to decide if/whether a trans person is sufficiently trans to receive treatment. However, when it comes to delivering that service, there is also a need for GP's and surgeons. But these are in short supply.

In part, because in certain well-upholstered quarters this is regarded as a pariah calling. Because, obviously no serious medic is going to want to treat those 'weirdo transes'! That is even before the active hostility – from colleagues and from anti-trans campaigners – that gender specialists can expect to receive. The media are very good at reporting alleged death threats made against prominent gender critical activists. Rather less diligent when it comes to reporting similar when the threats are directed at those trans allies.

Many of those who kept gender services going through the noughties and the twenty-tens have shipped out. The combined impact of age, retirement and, just generally, 'not needing the stress' any more.

Meanwhile, the supply of new specialists coming forward to replace those leaving is not so much pipeline, as trickle. Seeing just how much of a political football gender services have been made into over the past few years, who can blame them? After all, it is a rare bird who spends ten years plus, training to be a doctor, and then opts to martyr themselves in this way.

There truly are some amazing clinicians working within the system. Many genuinely have trans people's well-being at the heart of what they do. But they are working within a broken system.

There is incompetence. There is much general ill will towards trans people. There is, too, a continuation of previous nastiness. A suspicion that not everyone in the NHS – or even in gender services – sees helping trans people to a successful transition outcome as a valid goal!

Incompetence and under-funding

When it comes to basic incompetence, look no further than the case of the St Peters Andrology Centre contract. St Peters, for a long while, was the only facility in the UK offering NHS phalloplasty and metoidioplasty[25]. Also, the only facility fixing issues that arise with existing surgeries on their own patients.

These are complex surgeries. In many cases, more than one session is needed. So, trans men frequently undergo a first surgery on the understanding that it is just stage one. There may be discomfort – most commonly dysphoria – while waiting for stage two. Occasionally, though, where there are complications, actual pain. Still, it is understood that the gap between surgeries should not be too long. Because, in cases where there is a complication, delay can impact healing and eventual outcome.

Simply put: starting either of these procedures without a clear timeline for finishing them is a bad idea. In the worst-case scenario, patients may be forced to endure chronic pain for months. Years, even. Delay can adversely affect the end result.

25 Alternative procedures for creating a (neo-)penis for trans guys. If you want all the messy details, Google is your friend. (Other search engines are available!)

In March 2020, the Covid-19 pandemic led to a pause on surgical procedures across the NHS. As part of this pause, all non-emergency surgeries at St Peters were cancelled. So far, so ordinary. Less ordinary: on 31 March of that year, the contract between St Peters and NHS England was allowed to expire.

For the next 15 months or so, this service ceased to exist for trans men living in England. Also, in the Republic of Ireland, which sends patients to the NHS provider for this service. In August and September 2020, a small number of patients did manage to access NHS phalloplasty and metoidioplasty with St Peters. Whether or not this was entirely lawful – given the lack of contract – is one for the lawyers.

By mid-2021, as the NHS struggled back to life, the service remained in limbo. Though (official) news was slow to non-existent. Gender Clinics told some patients on waiting lists that the service was no more. Otherwise, information trickled out. In May, NHS Specialist Commissioning sent out a polite email informing patients that "we'll get back to you soon." In another, patients were told that an update was coming in July.

In fact, little more was heard until September, when the NHS belatedly announced that a contract to provide phallo and meta surgery had been awarded to the New Victoria Hospital. However, surgeries did not begin again until December. For priority patients. Those 'merely awaiting stage 2 or 3 surgery' had to wait until at least March 2022 before the list would open to them.

Since then, it would appear that some additional capacity

has been made available. At Chelsea and Westminster Hospital; and, briefly, at Parkside. Although Parkside never so much as started training the team. People were contacted and asked if they'd be willing to move onto the Parkside list. But that offer was retracted.

This is mostly positive. On the other hand, according to an FOI, lodged in February 2022, some 1,944 people were on NHS waiting lists for 'phallo and meta'. This compares to a target rate, set by the NHS, of 472 procedures per year; and an actual achieved operation rate of approx. 23 procedures a month.

You do the math! That's a four to five year waiting list. Even before you factor in that most individuals have several procedures. Or that, the more surgeries are done, the larger the excess load of patients coming back for revisions and adjustments.

Clearly, there is incompetence here. After all, it takes a certain advanced form of ineptitude, even in the midst of a pandemic, to allow a contract with the unique provider of a specialised service to lapse. But this is not just a one-off. Rather, it is long-term stuff, compounded by poor crisis management in 2021/2.

The time to be fixing this – training staff, putting in capacity – was not then, but ten years previous. Even so, there were stopgap solutions that the NHS might have resorted to, about which TransActual asked. Would they commission surgeries abroad? That might not have solved the immediate crisis. But it would have taken pressure off UK-based services.

Patients needed information. It was not forthcoming. Patients needed pain management. Because many were left in pain for months or years. They needed counselling. Because many patients reported a spike in their feelings of gender dysphoria while waiting. TransActual asked about these, too.

The NHS response? No apology. No acknowledgment that they had created these issues. Could they provide some dedicated support for those experiencing mental health issues due to the delay? Nope! Just a somewhat impractical suggestion that individuals could 'go back to their Gender Dysphoria Clinic for help.' Except anyone already discharged from their clinic cannot just go back and 'ask for support.'

This was not a pretty saga; and the NHS did not cover itself in glory.

Beyond the base incompetence is something else. It is hard to categorise. I would argue it is systemic. A failure to join things up.

So, not just under-funding, but poor handling of funds, and general incompetence. How much funding is needed? That's hard to tell. Though one clear yardstick is the waiting times (see above). To any stage of treatment. Whether you want a first appointment, or lower surgery, it is unlikely, now that you will be waiting less than multiple years.

So, a hysterectomy is typically provided – and centrally funded – if a patient is having it as part of their phallo and meta surgeries. Otherwise, as a stand-alone procedure, it is not centrally funded by the NHS. So, trans patients seeking hysterectomy (even if they are in agony with gynaecological issues) face a postcode lottery. Funding may be found in their area. It may not. That leaves a lot of people without access to hysterectomy and unable to have a vaginectomy.

Similar issues arise around electrolysis. Contrary to the views of some mainstream columnists this is not a purely cosmetic procedure. Genital electrolysis for trans women, for instance, is a prerequisite to lower surgery. A fixed amount of treatment is also available for facial hair removal through the NHS.

In practice, it, too, falls into the cracks between providers. No-one quite seems to be responsible for the budget for the latter. So, expect to be bounced around from place to place before being redirected to the start. In my own case, I gave up in frustration. I was entitled to a – wholly inadequate – 8hrs of laser or the cost equivalent of electrolysis... but it was just simpler, quicker, to go private.

Ill will

Meanwhile, the delivery of any sort of service to trans people is bedevilled with ill will. Though this is harder to substantiate. Because so much of it manifests out of sight. Or wrapped in a glossy outer layer of 'concern.' Occasionally it pokes its head above the parapet. As, for instance, in 2021, when a west country GP cited a notable anti-trans campaigner, claiming, on Twitter, that the trans vagina was an "open wound." This repeats a slur, often directed at trans women, that post surgery, the resulting 'neo-vagina' is a thing that can only be maintained by daily dilation. Otherwise, it 'heals up.' This is news to me, and to thousands of other trans women, who live our lives quite happily without additional intervention, from one month to the next!

Clearly, misinformation is a thing. However, there is a much subtler transphobia at work at every level within the NHS. Check out #Transdocfail[26], which still exists, both as hashtag and website somewhere out in the netsphere. It began with a spontaneous outpouring of trans anger and disgust with the medical profession. A response to what many saw as a General Medical Council vendetta against one trans-friendly medic, Dr Richard Curtis. It rapidly turned into a catalogue of indignities visited upon trans people by medical professionals at every level. Difficulties in obtaining treatment. Difficulties in continuing treatment. Hostility.

When it comes to abortion, the law provides GPs with a right to opt out. Though, you must still direct your patient to an alternative service provider. Your conscientious objection can never be excuse for actively denying treatment to anyone. There is no such opt-out when dealing with trans patients[27]. Or is there? The GMC warns doctors that they may not refuse medical services because a patient is "proposing to undergo, is

---

26 Belcher, H. (2014). *TransDocFail -The Findings Background.* [online] Available at: https://challengingjourneys.wordpress.com/wp-content/uploads/2014/11/transdocfail-findings.pdf [Accessed 26 Jul. 2024].

27 General Medical Council (n.d.). Religious and Personal Beliefs: Conscientious Objection. [online] https://www.gmc-uk.org. Available at: https://www.gmc-uk.org/education/standards-guidance-and-curricula/guidance/religious-and-personal-beliefs.

undergoing, or has undergone gender reassignment." Sorted!

Well, not quite. There is a loophole. (There is always a loophole!). Elsewhere[28], the GMC allows medics to refuse to provide – or to refer patients for – any services to which they hold a conscientious objection. Such as treatments that cause infertility. That is an interesting position. Some might say 'contradictory.' Because a full transition often implies infertility. So, perhaps GPs are allowed to refuse HRT? Because even if it does not cause infertility in and of itself, it is heading in that direction. Who knows? It is certainly 'wiggle room.'

In theory, the same standard should apply when it comes to treating trans patients as it does for doctors who have ideological objections to the termination of pregnancy. That is, they should refer the patient to a colleague who has no such objections. Otherwise, it brings into question their fitness to practice. But does it? In putting together this book, I have spoken to far too many individuals not granted this courtesy.

Many of the cases popping up in the 'fail' category were clearly transphobic. The individual denied treatment for a heart condition. Because with "all this gender stuff going on [..] it was probably in my head." An A&E practitioner insisting on a genital exam. Before a chest x-ray. For chest pain. So many genital exams! Suggested as addendum to conditions that go nowhere near the genitals. Surely, cis folk are not just weirdly curious

28 General Medical Council (n.d.). *Personal Beliefs and Medical Practice: Par. 8 (Conscientious objection).* [online] https://www.gmc-uk.org. Available at: https://www.gmc-uk.org/professional-standards/professional-standards-for-doctors/personal-beliefs-and-medical-practice/personal-beliefs-and-medical-practice#conscientious-objection.

about what trans folk keep in their knickers? Such cynicism!

The widespread assumption that almost every issue trans people present with is somehow a side-effect of HRT. Or psychosomatic: "because they were trans." Not forgetting 'trans broken arm syndrome.' That is, a tendency to swerve routine inquiries, about pretty much anything - from back ache to hearing loss - into discussion of gender and/or hormone treatment. In formal terms, this is called diagnostic overshadowing.

Even this pales into insignificance beside the outright abuse that many trans patients suffer just for being trans. Verbal abuse. An individual turned away at the reception of their local gynaecological clinic; described as "it" as they did so. A trans man told he only wanted to transition because he was too ugly to live as a woman. Yet another trans woman referred to as a "shemale" - for most trans people a highly insulting term - by their psychotherapist.

The individual told it was a shame how so much effort was put into trans treatment while there was no cure for cancer. The NHS Direct doctor who advised the partner of a trans individual to leave them. Because they were an "abomination."

The patient with a perforated appendix refused a wheelchair by hospital staff, and forced to walk to the operating theatre. Later, they learnt that that single piece of petty discrimination could have killed them.

Few and far between? Or tip of the iceberg? TransActual's

Trans Lives Survey 2021[29]is one of the largest dedicated research works looking at the experiences of trans people in the UK. It found 29% of respondents had been refused care because they were trans. 45% reported that their GP did not have a good understanding of the needs of trans people. In addition, 70% of respondents felt that they had been impacted by transphobia when accessing GP services. In similar vein, a 2018 survey from the charity Stonewall found that 32% of trans people reported unequal treatment by healthcare staff[30].

With such poor service, you might imagine that medical professionals would be falling over themselves to do better. Because who wants to spend half their working life fending off complaints? Well, yes. Except this is a service the GMC will happily provide for them. Following the TransDocFail project, over 200 specific instances of poor, sub-standard, sometimes downright dangerous treatment were forwarded to the GMC. They hemmed and they hawed. They whittled. Eventually they whittled 200-plus complaints down to just two. What became of these? I could not say.

A major part of the problem is systemic. There are myriad ways in which the current system geometry makes it difficult to provide treatment. Add in the levels of ill will highlighted above, and it is very hard to know why, in any given circumstance,

29 TransActual UK (2022). *Trans lives survey 2021: Enduring the UK's hostile environment.* [online] *https://www.transactual.org.uk/*. Available at: https://www.transactual.org.uk/trans-lives-21.

30 Stonewall. (2018). LGBT in Britain: Health Report. Available at: https://www.stonewall.org.uk/system/
files/lgbt_in_britain_health.pdf

a medical professional is being less than helpful. Are they transphobic? Genuinely sceptical of established treatments? Afraid of getting it wrong? Do they have conscientious objections? Or are they simply hemmed in by a service of such complexity, so many ill-fitting, constantly moving parts, one might conclude it was designed by Heath Robinson?

That would be insult to the good Mr Robinson. The over-riding feature of his weird and wonderful contraptions is not that they did not work. Rather, they resolved everyday issues through the design of over-elaborate and whimsical solutions. Fun, loveable stuff. The NHS, by contrast, provides over-elaborate solutions that are anything but whimsical – and in many instances fail to work well, transparently, or even at all. Not at all loveable.

Take referral to a gender clinic by a GP. This is no longer a requirement by all GICs. However, back when it was, examples abounded of GP's who simply refused to refer. Again, analysis of TransDocFail data highlighted how complaints about GP's and GP practices were far and away the largest category. Moreover, one of the main sources of complaint was around a refusal to treat or refer. When I wrote *Transition Denied*, a central part of the tragedy that befell Synestra was that her GP was not keen on referring her. So, for the best part of three years, he fobbed her off. The process was difficult. There were hurdles. He did not know how to fill out the forms. Likely she would have been waiting still on the day she died, had it not been for a trans masc friend who accompanied her to an appointment.

The usual excuses were coming thick and fast. Trans guy –

or hero, as I like to think of him – stepped up and placed a short form on the GP's desk. 'Fill that out!' (or words to that effect). GP, cornered, complied. A few months later, first appointment. Or it would have been. Except Synestra had died a week before the gender clinic letter came through.

More cunning were those who said they would refer – and then just happened to misplace the referral. As you will see from the transition stories, this was not uncommon. The first a trans person might know that they had NOT been referred to a clinic, was when they rang their practice, six months down the line, to inquire what the delay was. To be met with 'Referral? What referral?'

In the last decade, the battle lines have shifted. Now, it is all about the hormones.

For there are many roads to HRT; and for every road, its own peculiar roadblock. If you transition through the NHS then, sooner or later, you will likely be prescribed HRT. Or rather, the gender clinic recommends you receive HRT and/or hormone blockers. It is then up to the GP to write out the prescription. This is not rocket science. It is an approach that works well across a range of niche services.

Not so much when it comes to trans people. Stories abound of GP's refusing to administer or prescribe such treatment. Even where recommended by a GIC. Two reasons are regularly cited. The first, systemic, is to do with budget. Because gender clinics have not, historically, had the budget to pay for HRT. So, the spend must be borne by the GP practice.

The second, rather more nuanced, is that the GP claims to lack the specialist knowledge to go with the recommendation. This is basic. The legal position is set out on numerous practice websites. The person who signs a prescription is legally liable for the prescribing and the consequent effects of that drug. So, a GP cannot be compelled to prescribe a thing. Even where it comes endorsed by the relevant specialists up to and including endocrinologists.

Of course, by its very nature General Practice lacks specialist knowledge. It is expert in interdisciplinary general knowledge. Thus, Primary Care (GPs) refer to Secondary Care (General Hospitals) or Tertiary Care (Specialist Centres e.g. GIC). A necessary corollary to such referral is that they are expected to follow the advice that comes back.

Otherwise, apart from A&E, hospitals would get no patients. If the secondary or tertiary recommendation is for medicines, the GP is expected to follow that by prescribing them. If they really believe they have inadequate expertise or have ethical objections then they must pass the patient on to an appropriate colleague. It would also be reasonable to expect them to remedy their knowledge deficit as part of their continuing medical education and annual appraisal - otherwise their fitness to practice could be called into account.

Somewhere back of this is legal advice from organisations such as the Medical Defence Union urging caution. That's admirable. Also, very convenient. An easy figleaf for transphobia. Not least because there are also plenty of GP's who claim innocence in all matters trans. Yet they still have some very definite opinions on transitioning. Worse, as below, are those more than happy to intervene to block treatment. While still maintaining that transition is a complex topic of which they know nothing.

The stories of GP's either refusing to honour gender clinic recommendations, or tinkering with them are legion. In one case, a prescription for hormones was refused because of concerns that the patient was "not taking them safely." In another, a GP unilaterally reduced an individual's hormone dosage because they (the GP) decided that they needed greater libido. They didn't ask first!

Then there are 'bridging prescriptions.' These are 'temporary' prescriptions for HRT, issued to patients waiting specialist treatment. However, increased wait times at gender clinics have led to an increase in 'self-medding.' Trans people source HRT through a variety of channels, at varying degrees of risk. Relatively safe options include private clinics and independent online pharmacists. More risky are the dark web, and supply by friends.

Overall, though, it is seen as better all round for GP's to take over such prescribing. Bridging prescriptions provide reassurance that the HRT dispensed is in accordance with NHS standards. It is what it says on the package, and is not laced with dubious additives. Further, it is a prompt for GP's to include the patient in regular checks for any side-effects. Although, as at least one individual interviewed for this book has told me: GP's can also refuse to carry out such monitoring[31] because 'they do not have budget allocated for it.' This seems to be a system defect on the part of the NHS. Important services cannot happen if no budget is allocated.

Availability of bridging prescriptions is, though, very much luck of the draw. Some GP's will issue them. Some will not. Some agree to, but at the minimum dosage permissible. Some will only do so for three months. That might be fine if the gender service was working adequately and wait times were of similar order. However, with wait times of the order of several years, 3 months' HRT is not helpful.

In addition, following a dispute between NHS England and private clinic Gender GP, many GP's now refuse to pick up any prescriptions that originated with that group.

Then, there is the horrific - and dangerous - practice of GP's playing fast and loose with stable, existing HRT prescriptions. Why? After all, the basis of good medical practice is 'first, do no harm.' Whereas messing with something that is working well is the opposite of this. Over the years, I have heard stories of prescriptions changed. Prescriptions stopped. Sometimes after years on HRT.

This is especially an issue in respect of trans women. If the

---

31 Monitoring of HRT levels and associated issues is best carried out by an endocrinologist specialising in this area. That is, by a GIC. The alternative is the Welsh system, which uses a hub-and-spoke model with a central referral for assessment and initial HRT prescription.

Sub-regional services manage endocrinology (which takes about a year to settle down) initially. The patient is then referred on to specially-trained GPs to monitor and manage thereafter. Wales is a good example of how things can be made to work reasonably well.

individual is pre-op, an abrupt withdrawal can trigger symptoms that approximate to a menopause. It can impact mood. It can have serious effects on overall mental health. Though, of late, heightened 'debate' about how to treat trans people means many – even those long transitioned – are living in a constant state of anxiety. Worried, each and every day, that today might be the day that their GP 'turns sceptical.' It is something that politicians and columnists might do well to consider before placing yet another of their 'biens pensées' on transness into the wider public sphere.

Where an individual is post-op, withdrawal is disastrous. The body is adjusted to a new hormonal regime. Systems that might previously have produced other hormones no longer exist. So, all of the bad effects of withdrawal pre-op. And more. Post-op trans women, for instance, may find themselves rapidly descending into osteoporosis. Research is sketchy. However, according to specialists in the area, withdrawal can also lead to a slow – and painful – premature death.

Beyond HRT, if you can imagine a way that a GP can mess with treatment, someone, somewhere has probably done it. Refusal to write a letter stating a trans woman had had surgery? Check. Wholesale shredding of a patient's notes? Check. Even: "it's not dysphoria; it's your mother!" Honestly, I had not seen that one coming.

Why, then, dear reader, have you not heard these stories? Apart from the obvious? That mainstream media are mostly not interested in them.

The primary reason, as I wrote in the Introduction, is the law. I have tried on several occasions to expose GP bad practice. Most times, publications have just refused to publish. Because libel. Last time this happened, I wrote about a GP whose transphobia had, in my opinion, contributed to the death of a patient. I dropped them an email. Would they care to comment? Days later, the response. Short. Sweet. Print my name or any identifying details and... you will hear from my lawyers!

When it comes to trans people, there is an epidemic of abuse going on. But it is silent abuse. In the shadows abuse. Unless you are part of the trans community you will likely never hear of it.

While these may seem issues that impact 'binary trans' people, non-binary folks are also affected. This is because, as you will see in the individual stories, many non-binary individuals do opt for some hormonal intervention and/or surgery. However, acknowledgment of any genders outside 'the norm' appears to be difficult for many GP's. There is widespread refusal to discuss or acknowledge non-binary models of gender. In more than one instance, being non-binary was given as a reason for refusing HRT.

The nasty

If incompetence, and a certain amount of truculence on the part of service providers, was the worst that trans people faced, then life would be difficult. Nonetheless, with time, and insight, most problems can be solved. The bigger issue is existential. It goes to the heart of what you believe transness is.

I don't mean: 'let us get into the weeds' of this or that niche theory. Whether transness is expression of gene diversity. Or something to do with early years learning. Or even, according to one 'scientist,'[32] a sexual fetish for getting pleasure from the clothes one wears. It is a bizarre theory, a silly theory, which would apply and not apply in equal part to all women, cis and trans alike.

No. This is the fundamental question of whether you believe trans people are real. A genuine manifestation of human variability. Or some quirk of modern wokery. If you have got this far – and not skipped the sections on history – then you will know we are neither 'modern,' nor recent.

We are not 'being trans' for social kudos, public recognition or *because* we "know[s] it *teases*!"

From this an inexorable logic flows. If we are real, we need support. Not from a perspective of 'curing us.' Or putting us right. Rather, we need support to deal with the dysphoria. Also, to deal with the social pressures. The fact that for some trans people, just leaving the house is to invite abuse, both physical and verbal. Trans folk who have transitioned outside the UK tell how, in many countries, the gender service is not there to question them. Rather, it exists to support and talk through.

I explore just what is needed later on. After listening to many,

32 Autogynephilia.

many trans people. However, it should come as no surprise to learn that I will be suggesting that refusing treatment, trying to delay transition – whether young or old – will only do harm. Likewise, treating transness as second best. As 'tragedy;' or as an outcome to be avoided at all costs.

...and then it got really bad

Since c. 2020, life for trans people in the UK has become increasingly intolerable. It is underpinned by the constant construction of 'being trans' as not only a bad outcome but one that can be avoided. Because at some deep level, it is article of faith held by many cis people that transness is a 'choice.' A fad. Hence the decades-long privileging of non-empirical guesses by Freudian theorists over actual empirical evidence from doctors and trans people. Hence, too the fact that the last government decided at one point that trans people did not need protecting from conversion therapy. Because if you are trans – and especially if you are young and trans – then you have to demonstrate that you are very, very sure. Surer than when you join the army; get married; or terminate a pregnancy.

In 2019, NHS England put in place new National Service Specifications for Gender Identity Services for Adults. On the plus side, these finally prevented compulsory sterilisation. However, they also maintain trans psychopathologisation. Shiny new Gender Dysphoria Clinics [GDCs] must have 'expertise in mental healthcare needs that are specific to individuals with gender dysphoria.'[33]

Since these are not the general mental health needs that may attend anyone undergoing life-changing healthcare – anxiety, depression, stress – what can they be? Twenty years after government officially declared that being trans is not a mental illness, trans healthcare is still located in NHS mental health trusts. Not in ordinary district general hospitals.

A cis woman seeking HRT to support her mental health needs has only to mention this to her GP. Prescription follows. Whereas, a trans man, trans woman or non-binary person must undergo years of waiting. They must suffer intrusive therapy. At the end, they still cannot be sure of receiving treatment. Over the last couple of years, this position has become measurably worse.

This is reflected in almost every single aspect of the service provided within the NHS or by the wider political estate. It is further under-written by a continuing divide between the fine words issued by politicians of every stripe – and the seeming impossibility of pinning down anyone responsible for turning those words into practice. Take waiting lists. Again.

In 2022, the High Court rejected a challenge to NHS England over its failure to achieve anywhere close to an 18-week maximum delay for trans folks seeking medical treatment.

33 NHS England (2022). *Service specification: Gender Identity Services for Adults (Non-Surgical Interventions). v4.* [online] NHS England. Available at: https://www.england.nhs.uk/wp-content/uploads/2019/07/service-specification-gender-dysphoria-services-non-surgical-oct-2022.pdf.

Because, according to Lord Justice Popplewell: "NHS England's function is one of arranging. It cannot achieve a waiting time standard itself by the provision of services, but only by making arrangements designed to achieve it through the provision of services by others. Whether those arrangements do achieve it is not in NHS England's hands."

OK. The government sets waiting time targets. But no-one is quite responsible for delivering them.

Which is not to say that NHS England cannot act with alacrity when it wishes. In 2020, the High Court ruled it unlikely that a child aged 13 or less would be competent to give consent to the administration of puberty blockers[34]. Within hours of this ruling being handed down, NHS England issued an edict. This placed significant restrictions on the treatment of trans children until such time as they could put new guidelines in place. A year later, this ruling was over-turned on appeal. NHS England's reaction was anything but swift. In fact, the treatment of trans kids remained in much the same limbo as it had done before the appeal.

Meanwhile, government was setting up a review – under Dr Hilary Cass – designed, at least superficially, to seek out evidence of bad practice in the gender service for young trans people, and to assist in the generation of guidelines. On the surface, this was a project that the trans community should have welcomed. After all, one of the major criticisms that the Review later made

34 *Bell v Tavistock* [2020] (High Court) Available at: https://www.judiciary.uk/wp-content/uploads/2020/12/Bell-v-Tavistock-Judgment.pdf.

was the lack of a decent evidence base within the UK in respect of outcomes. This was something that the trans community had long been asking for. Except, Freudians – of whom there were many in the gender clinics – are not naturally disposed to such research. As this book has already suggested, there were many issues that the trans community had with existing gender services. So, a review that lifted the lid on what was happening, and that worked in tandem with the affected communities, could have been just what the doctor ordered.

Unfortunately, the Cass Review did none of this. Rather, it appears to have been commissioned by government with one eye to an agenda that included imposing severe restrictions on the ability of young trans folk to transition. This it delivered in spades!

It began by excluding trans individuals – experts and service users alike – from any governance role in the process. This is not standard practice for projects of this sort and led directly to some minor, but irritating misconceptions on the part of Cass about trans people. The case for such exclusion? Trans people might be biased!

OK. Possibly. Though the same argument could be used for excluding women from any review of pregnancy services. For excluding older people from any review of public transport for pensioners. And so on.

On the other hand, several of those included within the governance structure of the project held views that were at least supportive of conversion therapy. Even, perhaps, 'gender critical'[35].

Then, even more controversial, was the Review's approach to evidence. It is not quite as stark as claims made shortly after the release of the associated report that '98% of papers looked at had been excluded". However, it is fair to say, based on statements by the review team on release, and since, that much positive research was effectively excluded because the review process opted for a methodology and a standard for inclusion that was arbitrarily high relative to the questions asked.

Beyond this, academics have noted that it abounds with weird dog whistles to conspiracy theories created by overly-online transphobic bigots. There is no citation or evidence for its central finding that the rise in numbers is 'not explained by rise in social acceptance.' There is the continuing unevidenced claim that 'historically' most trans people were trans women. There is repetition of peer pressure myths promoted by the widely discredited theory of 'Rapid Onset Gender Dysphoria' (ROGD). This is a far from exhaustive list of Cass issues.

Nonetheless, the review concluded that there was insufficient evidence to justify prescribing puberty blockers to young trans people. So, the NHS issued yet another standard, instructing clinics not to prescribe.

The icing on the cake followed a few weeks later, in the closing hours of the 2019-24 parliament. Health Secretary Victoria Atkins issued a statutory instrument – effectively an

---

35 For a fuller background to the terminology, see Pearce, R., Erikainen, S. and Vincent, B. (2020). TERF wars: An introduction. The Sociological Review, [online] 68(4), pp.677–698. doi:https://doi.org/10.1177/0038026120934713.

executive decree – banning the prescribing of puberty blockers to young people in the UK. This is, of course, to 'close a loophole.' Because trans people, young and old, unable to obtain reliable medical treatment through the state, have been taking matters into their own hands and going private.

This, though, for a government that in almost every other respect is a fan of private medicine, is strangely intolerable. Every workaround that trans people find and exploit has been declared over the last few years a 'loophole' and in need of closing. Except, of course, that every time a loophole is closed, another opens. But with added danger and greater risk for the individuals involved.

This decree is effective for three months. So, it is anyone's guess what will happen longer term. However, since the current Health Secretary (Wes Streeting) has both declared his enthusiasm for such a ban, and defended it in court, it is likely here to stay. Besides, pharmacies were already wary of fulfilling prescriptions for trans people. Yes: one can obtain a legitimate prescription for HRT in the UK. But no-one is under any obligation to dispense it to you! There are therefore fears that even if this ban is lifted, it will be nigh on impossible to obtain puberty blockers legitimately in the UK.

In explaining her rationale for implementing this ban, Atkins made a seemingly odd reference to protecting children from the influence of pornography. Assuming this is not just random utterance, she appears to have picked up on musings by Cass based on a single paper that definitely does not meet the inclusion criteria for her review. This argues that one reason for children identifying as trans is porn. Does this make sense? Is it based on "quality" evidence? Not at all.

Certainly, no more than further musings from Cass in respect of SSRI's. These are a category of anti-depressant that are currently contra-indicated for young people. There is no evidence to support their use in the cohort that might otherwise receive puberty blockers. Though there is plenty of evidence to suggest they can be harmful. For this reason, they are not advised for prescribing to young people. But having delivered her central conclusions, which have since been parlayed up by politicians and media into supposed cast iron evidence that puberty blockers are harmful, none of this is surprising.

Meanwhile, the ban itself is intrinsically transphobic. How do we know this? During the pre-election period, politicians are supposed to restrict themselves to non-controversial initiatives. So, the risks from puberty blockers must be immense for Atkins to ignore the norms in order to impose an urgent ban on puberty blockers for trans kids. And therefore, also, for children with precocious puberty: the cohort for whom puberty blockers were initially developed? No. The ban applies only to puberty blockers prescribed to trans people. So, presumably, the risk lies not in the drug itself, but in the fact that some of those taking it might be trans.

Of course, none of this should come as surprise to those who have seen how supposed independent inquiries have been re-purposed by the last government. Various EHRC inquiries into racism in the UK, which have pretty much rejected systemic racism as a thing. Or the dearth of EHRC expertise and experience in respect of disability.

Or, as Preeti Kathrecha, a senior associate of the EHRC, and race-protected characteristic lead until 2021, put it, in evidence to a Tribunal at which she claimed unfair dismissal[36]:

> "The commission, which was supposed to be independent and impartial on race and other forms of discrimination, was politicised on some areas, such as race (and, more recently, the trans debate).
>
> "By politicised I mean that the board increasingly acted as an agent of the Conservative government and against parties or organisations which the government were opposed to, or were in conflict with, rather than impartially and independently, and in accordance with its statutory duties ... It is being used as a political weapon in a cultural race war."

Once upon a time, public inquiries in the UK were at least superficially independent. Whereas the last few years have seen the packing of public bodies – from the BBC, to the Charity Commission, to the EHRC – with individuals sympathetic to the government's anti-woke agenda. So, it is hardly surprising if the

36 Haththotuwa, S. (2023). UK equality watchdog won't let staff say 'institutional racism', tribunal hears. *HR Grapevine*. [online] 6 Oct. Available at: https://www.hrgrapevine.com/content/article/2023-10-05-uk-equality-watchdog-wont-let-staff-say-institutional-racism.

output is anti-woke.

International reaction to the Cass Review has been muted. For the most part, though, those with expertise in the field have dismissed it as 'a nothing burger.' The Yale School of Medicine – hardly a bastion of woke liberalism - conclude that the review 'repeatedly misuses data and violates its own evidentiary standards by resting many conclusions on speculation'[37].

Meanwhile, the reaction from the World Professional Association for Transgender Health[38] (WPATH: formerly the Harry Benjamin International Gender Dysphoria Association) has been scathing. They eviscerate the Review for equating "negligible prior knowledge or clinical experience of trans and gender diverse youth" on the part of the report's author with "independence." They condemn how "ignorance of gender dysphoria medicine was framed as a virtue." They do not consider the Cass recommendations as worthy of serious consideration.

They also express serious concerns regarding the ethics of suggesting that puberty-blocking agents for young people in the United Kingdom might be available only in the context of a research protocol. This protocol has not been superseded by the ban. Rather, it's a highly manipulative form of arm-twisting.

---

37 McNamara, M., Baker, K., et al. (2024). *An Evidence-Based Critique of 'The Cass Review' on Gender-affirming Care for Adolescent Gender Dysphoria*. [online] Available at: https://law.yale.edu/sites/default/files/documents/integrity-project_cass-response.pdf.

38 WPATH and USPATH (2024). *WPATH and USPATH comment on the Cass Review*. Available at: https://www.wpath.org/media/cms/Documents/Public%20Policies/2024/17.05.24%20Response%20Cass%20Review%20FINAL%20with%20ed%20note.pdf.

For, faced with high degrees of potential opt-outs from the research, government is now banning access to private and overseas prescribers. So, in essence, if you want access to puberty blockers in future you will be forced to take part in an as yet non-existent research programme. Ethical? Not remotely.

Not that this international criticism will be especially surprising to Cass, or particularly concerning. For implicit in the review at various points is the view that no-one anywhere has done any research that is good enough. So, we Brits will have to roll up our sleeves and sort it all out. The gifted amateur rides again – and has since received a seat in the House of Lords for her pains.

Beyond this, the review process reveals two concerning threads that seem to underpin this take on trans healthcare. The first is epistemological. The second, ideological – and profoundly dangerous to the continuation of modern medicine in the UK.

Let's start with a small detour, by way of Liverpool Women's Hospital. It is one of the UK's leading maternity facilities. Yet, here, according to a significant peer-reviewed paper[39] in 2010, some 75% of drugs prescribed to folks during pregnancy were "off-label". Of those, 55% were "cautioned or contraindicated for use in pregnancy".

Worse still, a "significant number of these prescriptions"

39 *Herring, C., McManus, A. and Weeks, A. (2010). Off-label prescribing during pregnancy in the UK: an analysis of 18000 prescriptions in Liverpool Women's Hospital. International Journal of Pharmacy Practice, 18(4), pp.226–229. doi:https://doi.org/10.1211/ijpp.18.04.0007.*

were not just off-label, but high risk. That's 38 drugs (16% of total) and 1,735 (10%) of the total prescriptions.

See Table I below, and accompanying illustration.

	Drugs		Patients	
	Cases	**Percent**	**Cases**	**Percent**
Licensed for use in pregnancy	37	15.9%	4445	25.4%
Off-label but considered safe by the manufacturers	57	24.6%	3363	19.2%
Cautioned or cointraindicated by the manufacturer in pregnancy	138	59.5%	9722	55.5%
Total	232		17530	
High risk off-label	38	16.4%	1735	9.9%

Table I: Evaluation of prescribing to pregnant individuals in Liverpool Women's Hospital, IJJP (2010)

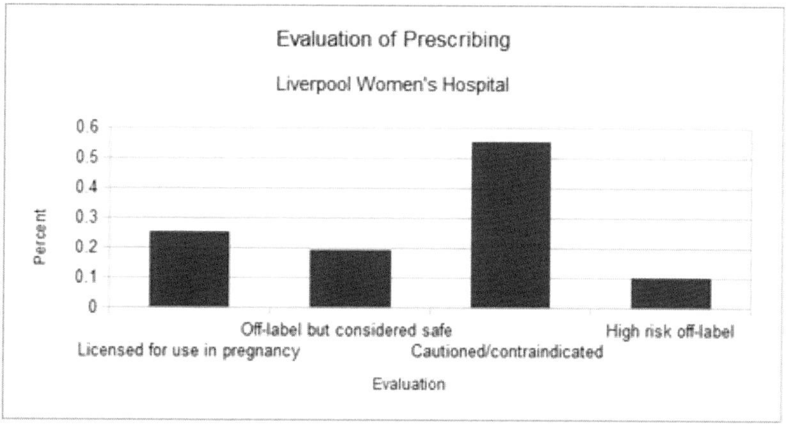

Illus I: Evaluation of prescribing to pregnant individuals in Liverpool Women's Hospital, IJJP (2010)

This, though is not system bug, but design feature. It is current practice, for reasons that are both ethics and cost-related, in respect of two highly vulnerable cohorts. Ethical, because informed consent is difficult to obtain in respect of children; and there are serious ethical concerns about testing out new drugs on pregnant people. Cost, because in evaluating a new drug, pharmaceutical companies explore principal uses. However, they cannot afford to explore all possible uses.

That's OK, though. Because current medical practice is to release new drugs, and pioneer new practice in accordance with what research has been done. Then, gradually to expand out from that base as additional research becomes available.

To demand the level of certainty for NHS prescribing generally that Cass has seen fit to require for puberty blockers for trans youth, would be to throw out somewhere between half and three-quarters of drugs currently prescribed.

In other words, to apply the Cass standard would require a radical re-structuring of the way we do healthcare in the UK more widely. Or, as the hospital study somewhat elliptically comments: "prescribers need to be aware of the risks associated with these drugs and the possible legal consequences of prescribing and administering them."

There is, though, something else, even more dangerous buried in the heart of Cass. This is the demand for more evidence – certainty, perhaps – before she can endorse the prescribing of puberty blockers. This goes well beyond the quibble about individual drugs and prescribing regimes; goes to the heart of how we should do medicine. Since Cass published, I have seen this attitude worm its way into other papers regarding trans healthcare.

There is 'no evidence of benefit.' Corollary: there might be harm. We 'just don't know.' This an extreme sceptical position. Applied more widely, it would stop all sorts of development in its tracks. Not just medicine. But wider technology, too.

Or is this just a concern that is applied to trans people? Surely not.

To be fair, the rhetoric of 'evidence-based policy/medicine' often is a blocker on anything new occurring because it hasn't already happened at scale in a perfectly controlled laboratory using spherical test subjects in a vacuum. Cass does appear to acknowledge the tension between progressing medicine and the requirement for evidence showing safety. However, the end result of her review comes down firmly on the side of pause.

The ideological nature of Cass is highlighted by what has followed. In quick succession after, the NHS announced a consultation on its ten-year constitution. Nothing especially unusual about that. It is standard practice to review the constitution every ten years or so. What is unusual - quite possibly a breach of the Equality Act and of the human rights of trans people - is the fact that it proposes a new right for patients to be treated only by individuals of the same "biological sex" as them. Further, it proposes the removal of trans women from women's wards. Presumably to side rooms. Given the shortage of beds in the NHS right now, this is unlikely to go down well with already hard-pressed hospitals.

However, the political nature of this proposal can be gauged by the fact that outside the frothing of various national news commentators, there is no evidence of any harm befalling ("biological") women from this exposure to the trans variety. How do we know? Trans organisation Translucent spent the best part of a year sending FOIs to NHS hospitals asking for details of any incident involving trans women on women's wards. The result? One complaint. As best can be told, this is merely objection to sharing space with a trans woman. Nothing more.

No evidence! Where is that Cass standard of proof when it might come in handy?

At the same time, the Royal College of General Practitioners issued revised guidance to GP's reminding them they did not have to support trans patients. Whether by means of bridging prescriptions, blood tests, or even prescribing drugs recommended. This has always been the case. However, this sort of public utterance, combined with high profile news stories like the ban on puberty blockers, the misdirection around the Cass Review, and the proposals for the NHS constitution set the mood music.

Pharmacies will be less inclined to fill trans-related prescriptions. GP's and other health professionals – even those sympathetic to trans people – will be more nervous about being supportive. Meanwhile, those already sceptic, hostile, will be emboldened to refuse treatment altogether.

We have seen this sort of thing happen in Italy, in respect of abortion services. Because while every woman has the right to an abortion, obstetric specialists also have a right to an ethical objection; to say no. So, in parts of (Southern) Italy, women have an absolute right to an abortion. In theory. In practice, they must contend with c.95% of obstetricians refusing to provide such service.

Are we headed that way in the UK? There is already significant and chilling evidence of general practitioners stopping prescriptions for trans people. First, do no harm? In some instances, an abrupt stop on HRT can be actively dangerous. However, that does not seem to bother some medical practitioners.

The result? Increasing distress and anxiety on the part of trans people. More, and more dangerous 'loopholes' opened up, as individuals scramble to avoid being forcibly detransitioned. Fear.

If you have read this far, I would leave you with a simple question. Are we, as the UK, not better than this? On present evidence, the answer is a resounding 'no'!

Beware the Gender Watch, my child!
Its forms who chide and scheme and spit!
Its claws click-clack some vile spew, a brew
of pseudo truths, and norms borne
long 'fore you and I.

Beware its white cloak and nib!
Its eyes that judge, its tongue that bites!
Beware its laws, of its degree!
That which brings shame on our family.

Beware its legions, of its beating drum!
Beware its rifle and bayonet –
its blade is stained, it's shells aplenty,
and there's no space for faith in our NHS.

Beware its binary, my child!
It's a tool that's out of order.
The Watch will hunt for its sake,
though its rules are true no longer.

Gender Watching, by Dorian Rose

Transition Stories: III

Quinn: The unexpected Brummie

Like many trans people, Quinn, 42 and non-binary, is facing mixed emotions following personal loss. Because, on the one hand, losing someone close to you is never great. Yet, sometimes, it can free you up to make changes in your life you never dared to before.

Certainly, that was my own experience. I'd have loved my mum to meet and understand the transitioning me. At the same time, I have always wondered. Would I have dared transition while she was still alive? How would I have broken the news? Could I have?

Thus it is for Quinn. They tell me: "I am a photographer. I have my own business. I have also had to cope with a lot of death recently. My mum, my aunt, and my gran. All from cancer. That has meant change. A move from London to Birmingham is on the cards in the near future, along with recently becoming actively single and sober.

"It has also given me a certain freedom to follow the life I want. I can get tattoos. More seriously, I now have the space to come out as non-binary trans-masc.

"The people I cared about are not here. So, I can be me.

"I knew myself as queer from an early age. The result of mum raising me in York against a background of feminism, left politics, and the miner's strike. She didn't so much raise me genderless, as do so in a way that empowered women. If one can do it, anyone can do it. She was a single mum. So, I was treated early on like on adult. We shared in looking after the home. If I wanted to wear trousers, that wasn't an issue.

"Mum was pretty scathing of the 'pink pound.' That was back in the day before it picked up its LGBT connotations; when products branded as 'for women' typically cost more. Like razor blades. Or deodorant. So, I grew up as a tomboy: running, jumping, and climbing trees! That all worked fine. Except later there were consequences, as I found I did not fit in to a gendered society.

"When I was younger, I think my approach to society was quaint, old-fashioned. I got my first boyfriend at 16. In my 20s I tried very hard to conform. I became a femme caricature. I would not enter a shop without loads of make-up, and dressed very feminine.

"That lasted until about ten years ago. It was a pretty stereotypical rebellion against my mum. She did not wear make-up; had hairy legs; all the clichés! She was a punk. She'd turn up at school wearing a leather jacket, and smoking. Very much out there with her hair. You get the picture? Also, she was the sort of person who might be classified as being under the 'terf umbrella' now.

"Then, slowly, change started to filter through. I didn't come out as gay until I was over 30.

"Mum was not happy. She was fine with people being gay.

Just so long as that did not include her daughter. When I came out, I changed my Facebook status to 'in a relationship.' Mum's side of family all started asking questions. 'Who's this?' 'What's going on?'

"Then, when I met my wife in 2013, that was a wake-up call. I'd abandoned my old tomboy ways. She reminded me of who I had once been. For instance, she only wore make-up at special occasions. She told me: 'Don't bother wearing make-up.' So gradually I grew in confidence. Four years on, I'd stopped wearing it. I cut my hair. I changed from a 'normal' bra to a sports one. I'd wear my wife's clothes. Still, it was difficult not to hear my mum's voice inside my head, challenging me.

"We became estranged, and that continued, off and on, for many years. I think I always hoped for a reconciliation. That will never happen now. Mum was 62 when she passed.

"My gran was more conventional. Though she did divorce in an era when women did not divorce. So, she was a mixture. Conventional in marrying, and lived a married life. Unconventional in other respects. Before she passed, she told me to pick up a camera and make her proud. So, I sold my old equipment. I learnt what digital photography was; and then sat down to grieve for gran.

"I was not so close to my aunt. Still, the fact that three women had gone from my life in such a short space of time had an impact. My aunt, like my mum, was in her 60s. My gran was in her in 80s.

"Losing them started me on a personal journey, or crisis, of my own. I went through a phase of thinking I only had 20 years left to live. I decided I needed to change, and to take back my life. Over the years I have done many different jobs. Here and abroad. I was also, now, my wife's full-time carer from 2016 up until April2020.

Then, Covid came when we separated permanently. We tried couples therapy to reconnect but, in the end, separation was the best-case outcome. I had become a shell of who I was and incredibly isolated as my friends and family slowly dissipated, not fully understanding what I was going through.

"2020, I spent Christmas alone. My gran had passed. It was just me in the flat. F*ck that! I didn't want to be either gender. I wanted more tattoos! Why not? I also really enjoyed Covid. Because it gave me some peace and quiet and time to think. I began to ask 'who am I? 'I started to think about non-binary. What does non-binary mean? For me, it was about looking at what society expects from someone who is female or male. How it expects you to act or behave a certain way. Ultimately, how a lot of hate follows if you fail to conform.

"I knew I was not binary. I just wanted to be me, without all the pressure of conforming

"I researched the hell out of everything. I still am. I signed on with a gender clinic. At the same time, I used my inheritance to go private and I got a diagnosis of gender dysphoria. I started on testosterone, and have been on it now for about six months.

"When I discovered it was a possibility, I knew it was for me.

Mixed emotions. I knew it would have pissed off mum and gran. I also knew it was exactly what I needed to do. I weighed up the possible negative effects. I also knew that if I tried it and it did not work for me, I could back away.

"But I do not want to come off. It helps me to finally feel right in my skin and helps against my dysphoria and with my mental wellbeing. I'm on 3 pumps of testogel daily and it feels like this is how I should always have felt.

I don't have acne or hair in weird places, or anger issues. Just positive changes, including confidence, feeling more at ease in the world, and astronomical orgasms - which were always very good, but now are mind blowing! Since starting on testosterone, I regularly bind and pack and have been exploring 'STPs.' These are prosthetics that allow trans guys to stand to pee.

I'm also planning on getting top surgery at some point when I can afford it. But first, let's see what muscles I can gain at the gym now I have more energy. My muscle fat is naturally redistributing. So, now I want to see what I can do with this body and how I can make it work for me. Rather than suffer inside it.

"After all that – Covid, and splitting up and lots of loss – I went on tinder. I got involved in poly and the kink life started up. I've always identified as a 'butch dyke' or a 'leather dyke.' I rarely chat to my mum's family or friends. They dropped away over the years; and the main people whose views I cared about have passed on.

So, now there are people in my life who just know me as me...

tattooed, non-binary, Quinn.

"The result was pretty visible when I had a naming party last February. It was to celebrate my change of name. I invited old friends and family. But no-one came from that side of my life. It was an olive branch and I am nurturing friendships I have found.

"I came out as pansexual at about the same time. My gender and sexual orientation have both changed. Recently, I stopped all my relationships, because I needed to go sober and go single. I wanted to heal myself and take the business forward. I do events, family shots, portraits, boudoir, kink, corporate... and weddings. Let me know if you need a photographer!"

Zak: Just an everyday trans guy

Zak is fine, now. Though, over the years, he has suffered from health issues. Also, he is turning 39 soon. Probably already turned by the time this book is published. Although, he tells me, "Most people think I'm 28." Something to do with the 'curse' of youthfulness that trans people are gifted with.

Zak volunteers. He does not work, as he has an autoimmune disorder. "I think I had the autoimmune condition from very small. But it wasn't until I was 15 that I got a diagnosis. Granulomatosis with polyangiitis. Otherwise known as GPA for short. No-one else in the family has it. And I was recently diagnosed as autistic.

"I used to do retail. My first ever job was working in a preschool. But small kids have loads of bugs, so that did not go well. My nephews, too, were always going down with something. It means I get ill a lot. I suffer from chronic pain, fatigue. I have a stent in my chest and lung, because of scarring around the tube in my left lung. So, I don't get out much.

"As far as transition goes, I came out 2014. I got on the waiting list just in time.

"I think I always knew, from when I was quite young: 4, 5, maybe 6. I remember asking about it at the time, but people just brushed me off. They told me 'You're a girl, get over it.' I was confused. I didn't understand why I wasn't allowed to be a boy. It just seemed right. Natural.

"At school, though, there wasn't all that much education about LG or B, let alone T. I didn't raise it again. When I was in my teen years, about 13, my parents split up. Then, about two years later, I got my AID diagnosis. There wasn't room for anything else in my life. So, I parked my questions. I was already getting bullied a lot at school, anyway. Pretty much from the day I arrived to the day I left. I was just an odd person and an easy target. I'd always been small; also, quite quiet.

"I think there was also some sense of difference. In secondary school, I was friends with a lot of boys in my set, and that made other girls jealous. Only, I wanted to be 'one of them,' as opposed to being *with* them. For a while, at school, I dated boys, but I didn't much like it. Besides, dating women was loads better; though I did not come out as gay until my early 20s. Whatever the reason, I needed to survive and I needed to get out.

"Towards the end of 2013, in my late 20s, gender issues started to rear their head again. I decided to come out as non-binary for a bit, while I was thinking about stuff. Only 'they/them' just did not feel right. 'He/him,' on the other hand, seemed to fit me well.

"Family reaction has been mixed. Though, given I'm from Poole in Dorset, which is very Tory dominated, I'd say I've been lucky in how those closest to me have responded. My dad died in 2011, so he never knew. My mum's approach is not to speak about it. She is disappointed she doesn't have a girl any more; but I was never a 'girly girl.' I have a brother, who asks what seem very strange questions to me. Like 'can you get someone pregnant?' To me! He genuinely did not know. I guess it's a valid question if you don't know much about biology, and I am open to any and all questions. I've said to people, 'If you want to ask a question, go for it.' I think it comes from a place of love and fascination.

"I also have five nephews. When I told the oldest, he just went: 'OK. I like you better as a boy.' Mostly, though, he does not care. But kids are like that. Kids are mostly 'if you're going to give me food, that's fine.' People who worry are all like 'What about the children?' But so long as you explain simply, honestly, children do not care. They just get on with stuff.

"My mum's parents are still around, and they are not too bad. They call me Zak and for the most part remember to use he/him pronouns.

"I applied to the NHS in 2014. They saw me two years later;

in London, because that was easier to get to than Exeter. From Dorset! It was pretty straightforward. Before, I went up to a conference at Charing Cross. There were speakers; loads of people who had been referred around the same time. So, we just spent a day, an afternoon, just chilling; talking about hormones, surgery, everything.

"I got HRT in 2017. It felt really wonderful. I didn't want to start out with gel, because I know it takes time to work. I am also not too fond of getting spotty. Because my skin reacts after a while. So, it was on to injections straight away. There was a bit of delay in getting the paperwork sorted. No-one could sign until my endo got back from paternity leave. Another three months' delay.

"Still, I think it went smoothly because I knew what I wanted. Also, because I'd already been through the mental health system, they knew I was not schizophrenic or suffering from some other condition.

"Top surgery was the end of 2019. I'm still waiting on lower surgery; have been waiting for four years already. But I'm glad to have got as far as I have got. The dysphoria I feel for bottom surgery is not as bad as it was for top surgery. So, it's more manageable. All the same, I'd like to get it done before I turn 40. If not sooner.

"I got my second yes for lower surgery in 2020, but they did not put me on the list until 2022. First, because they stopped operating during Covid, which was standard. Then, because the NHS allowed their contract for this service to lapse, and it took them about a year to sort things out. Not so standard.

"In 2022, they renewed my referral. I emailed them a couple of weeks ago to ask what was going on, and they could not even tell me how long the waiting list was. But I have a friend who went on the list in 2019; and they have only just had bottom surgery in 2023.

"So, there is nothing for it but to wait. It's a complicated surgery; not as straightforward as MTF surgery. It can take three or four surgeries to get it all done. That means you can customise, and that's cool. It makes sense that you need certain things done within a certain amount of time. Though it is still a bit frustrating."

Has there been any pushback? Did Zak have regrets? "God no. I regret not doing it sooner. That's the only thing. Puberty was horrendous. Girls were all excited for bras and periods and stuff, and there I was going just 'Why?' Pretending to be excited too.

"Whereas now it just feels like how it is supposed to be. I think I have only just started to grow in confidence in the last year. I used to be quite shy. Now, though, I am more confident, and getting more so with every passing month.

"On the other hand, that sets the bar low, in terms of what counts as a good transition. I am a little worried about hate. There is a gay area in Bournemouth. I went out there in, I think, 2021. Another trans guy went there, and was assaulted by a couple of cis guys. The police didn't do anything. They said 'not enough evidence,' so that was that.

"It is possible it happened in the Bournemouth triangle outside the bar. There was no CCTV evidence. So, it was his word against everyone else's. Obviously, there was evidence he had been beaten up. but no identification.

"He was a trans man over here for university. From Spain, I think; and that may have been part of the reason for the assault. Transphobia, with added racism. It is the times we live in."

Nix: Dragon brings the magic

At 36, Nix is proud of what they have achieved. Not just in coming out and living life as non-binary. Also, bringing up three kids as a single parent, despite some pretty major challenges. They explain: "I am disabled, so I cannot work. The main issue is ME. It started after my first pregnancy, when I was 19 and it has got worse over the years, since. I've been lucky in that most of the medical support I have received has been positive. But there is not much support out there...

"So, I do stuff at home. I look after my kids, do some hobbies, do some writing. Mostly, it's YA fantasy (young adult). Odd stories, some set in this world, some in made-up worlds. I've done a zombie story. Then, in another kids are taken to another world that is split into different areas. One by one, the areas are being transformed into darkness, and they have to try and fix it. Mostly I lean towards magic in what I write."

Nix's eldest is at college now. But they also have a 10-year-old and an 8-year-old.

Like many trans people, Nix came out long after they knew. "I came out when I was around 30. I realised I was asexual and aromantic. Also, I always knew I was not a girl or boy. Still, when I came across 'non-binary,' there were loads of terms but none of them were quite right. It took me a while to find 'agender,' but it definitely fits.

"I mostly did not have explicit gender issues with my parents and school. For me there wasn't an issue, and I just got on with my life. People always label you. So, from before puberty, I figured when people say 'You're a girl,' it was 'Whatever.' The term was meaningless to me: redundant. Something projected onto me by others.

"Still, I guess you could say I had dysphoria during puberty, in the sense that I felt set aside from my gender. My body was gendering me. But, as a person, I had no gender. I was constantly going 'stop I don't want this,' but I had no sense that there was anything anyone could do about it.

"Too, my mum used to try and put me in dresses and skirts and I would have a meltdown. I hated being pigeonholed clothing wise. Now, I wear what I want and I like what I wear.

"Then it was off to college. I'm from the north. So, I went to a northern college. Small. But I was able to start a university course while I was there. I worked for a bit; got pregnant. A cliché, I guess: pregnant at 19 after a one-night-stand on holiday. A few months after that, I went back to do a business course. And I didn't finish the course. Too much happening, including the onset of ME. It wasn't too bad to start with. But it got worse when I was in my late 20s. Then I got long Covid; and after that, I was diagnosed with asthma.

"When I was 24, I met my future husband. Though that did not work out too well! While we were together, I had two more kids, when I was 26 and 28. We got married a year later; and I left him a year after that.

"The problem was he had mental health issues. But he was also controlling and abusive, and he brainwashed me into thinking I was the problem. My childhood wasn't great. He was the first to pay real attention to me; and he twisted everything round to make me feel he was helping family. Also, we'd been planning to get married for so long. We'd already been 'on the marriage train' for so long, I didn't feel I could back away.

"Most of the abuse was verbal, not physical. Though he did abuse my eldest a bit and towards the end it got worse. He would orchestrate issues with family and friends and go 'Look⊠ these people don't care for us.' So, he moved us further away from friends; out into the country. I had no money of my own. No transport. It was just one red flag after another.

"Then, he did start to threaten me physically. He also tried to push me towards wearing clothes that were frilly and feminine; wanted me to grow my hair out. But if I wasn't going to conform for my mum, I wasn't going to do so for him.

"I knew something had to change. I had to get out of there, and Social Services helped us escape. The local council sent a taxi to pick up me and the kids. We had one suitcase and not much more, so we lost a load of stuff. I did try to get some of it back. The Council were able to send a van once. But he refused access, and sent our things to a charity shop. He seemed to think that if he held on to our property, I might change my mind. It was also about being petty and controlling. He did not even let the kids have their belongings.

"For a while, we stayed in the area. Now we've changed counties. We were homeless for a bit, and I decided it was just easier to find somewhere to live somewhere new, than return to my home town and be homeless there. Relations with my family are not great; so, I can't count on any support there. Another thing that my husband made worse.

"Because I never had a great relationship with mum, and she did not like my ex. She had a hissy fit when he moved us away, and he orchestrated arguments between us. I've tried to get back in touch with her; but now, she's coming up with stories that are just not true. My step-dad is OK, but he won't do anything mum does not want. I did manage to get back in touch with my father when I was an adult, but he has his own family, and wasn't too interested.

"On the plus side, I've been here for the past 6 years, looking after my kids. I have no contact with the ex. I've changed my phone number, and he is blocked on social media. He does not know where we live and has no way to get in touch. So, we've had no need for a restraining order.

"I didn't really address the gender thing until after separating. I did try to explain 'asexual' to my partner when we were still together. He did not get it; and I felt it was not really worth explaining it to him. He was like 'You're in a relationship and married so obviously you are attracted to me.' He never listened. Pretty much talking to a brick wall.

"I came out to various people online. I'm slowly sorting out a name change. I'd already changed it once, when I got married – though just the last name. Later, when I left my ex, I changed first and last. It follows an email address I came up with at college, and which I've been using online ever since. I always liked Nix, though never with a 'c.' I also like dragons, and I have been much inspired by dragon lore through my transition.

"Anyway, I've changed my name now. But it's such a faff. I have had to do it at the doctor's, the dentist, the bank, and so on. I've caught the most important ones now but it's not changed everywhere, and I still have loads of stuff in my old name coming through.

"I've not taken any hormones. Don't plan to, because they would simply change my body to something else that I do not want. On the other hand, I do want top surgery. But I am going to wait until the kids are grown up first. The risks are low, but I have concerns about my overall health, so I don't want to take that risk until the kids are old enough to look after themselves.

"Being non-binary does not tend to have a massive impact, apart from the odd issues that arise in a gendered society. For instance, doing a quiz, I was asked to click 'male or female.' It's no big issue, but it still feels intrusive.

"The kids have been fine with it. In fact, questioning gender seem to run in the family. The eldest is a trans girl. The middle is gender fluid. The youngest is a boy. So far. They help out and support a little. But mostly not. I cannot expect them to do much as they struggle enough as it is. They are also autistic.

"Most people have been accepting. Though one Facebook friend was a bit scathing. She was all 'Why are you telling people about your gender? I'm lesbian and I don't go round telling people. 'I'm not sure if this was her not liking me, or ⊠but not like me talking about anything to do with my life. I have no idea why she had an issue, and I was like 'Well, that's your choice.'

"Otherwise, I'm doing OK. I get out to local prides and I have picked up a few flags. Non-binary flags!

"Also, over the last couple of years, I have been doing therapy to work out why I didn't do anything about this; because at the time, I did not understand what was happening."

CYK: A long and winding road

Some trans folks walk a harder road than others. CYK, now 46, non-binary and a therapist might not have taken the hardest road. But being brought up as an Orthodox Jew – albeit now secular – and discovering, at an early age, that you are queer, is certainly not the easiest.

CYK is London, through and through. They grew up in Brent, swapped home for life in south London when they were around 20. Then, Brighton. South-East London. And finally, back to North London.

They say: "When I came out, my family were good. At the time I was an Orthodox Jew mainly as I was still living at home with my family. For a while, I worked as a chef, and this led to my first accidental coming out as gay to my Mum. It was 1995; I was 17".

"For some reason, I always manged to get Friday and Saturday nights off. I have no idea how I managed that, as these were the busiest nights of the week in the restaurant. One afternoon I went to have a siesta. One of waiters left a message about going to Heaven Nightclub on the answerphone.

"Mum went: 'I think there's been an urgent message from work.' She started listening. Halfway through, she was crying. We talked. I wasn't really prepared to come out. I assumed what she needed to hear, I promised I would never get HIV and would do my best to have grandchildren."

Aged 17, I met my first boyfriend. It was likely he already had HIV. Within six months of being together he found out he had full-blown AIDS. It was horrendous. This was the catalyst that told me I needed to come out."

"That, though, was how she found out. At the time, she also said 'Don't tell dad: he would not agree with it.' So, I didn't, until a second accident forced my hand."

"A year or so later, I was interviewed in town about being an Orthodox and coming out as queer. I typed something out on my dad's work computer. At the end of the session, I thought I'd deleted it. Only I hadn't. My dad read it. You can guess what happened next. There was a big argument between my parents.

But I was lucky in more ways than one. Because in what I typed I said that if ever my dad found out I would be ostracised and homeless. When the argument died down, I went back to sleep. At 4.30am I was woken by something heavy at the end of my bed. I woke up to my father sitting at the end of my bed crying. When I came round, he said 'We will never kick you out and we will never ostracise you.' Indeed, the next day he went to work, found a Jewish LGBT inclusive synagogue, the then Jewish Gay and Lesbian Group, and Chofetz Chaim, an Orthodox Jewish Friday night service followed by dinner.

"My parents always felt that everyone should be welcome at the family table."

"My sister has always been good. Although her religious views have waxed and waned over the years. At one point, she was more secular. Then she became much more religious. That complicated matters a bit. But she has always attempted to be as open-minded as possible."

"It was not all so straightforward. When I went out into my parents' community, I would often have to pretend I was straight. My grandparents were never told I was queer and I was told they would ask too many questions and it may have negative consequences on their health due to their age. Though it was obvious something was up. No-one ever asked about partners. When I was about 30, one aunt kept trying to match-make for me, inviting me over on Friday evenings. I phoned my mum. I said: someone has to tell her that I am queer, and this is not fair to everyone, including the young women.

"Mother called. She told my aunt it would be lovely for me to meet a nice young woman 'as a friend.' But you need to know [CYK] is gay and nothing is going to happen. My aunt responded: 'I've got two brown eyes. Does it matter?' She was very accepting.

"I say 'gay.' Even then, though, I knew myself as queer, which was very much in tune with the 90s. Most of my friends were on the gender diverse spectrum. It just felt natural to connect with that. We did not have the language of queer or non-binary at this time.

"After working as a chef, I moved into first class catering. After that, I ended up as assistant reception manager at a hotel. One Christmas I was dealing with a huge line of people queuing. It was then that I realised I wanted to do something very different with my life. My brother has autism and I always volunteered in helping people with learning difficulties.

"I went back and did an access course into social work and social care. Then I moved into LGBT school liaison work and working with young LGBT people through LGBT youth support services. After eight years of that and having had a good experience of therapy myself, I decided to move on from working with young people.

On my intermediate training there was a lot of homophobia. The course tutor asked me to keep their lesbian identity a secret and all of this did not make the course feel so safe. I completed my Level 4 Counselling Diploma in 2008 and have now been a therapist for about 15 years. I did a psychodynamic and intercultural – also known as transcultural – diploma (no, not 'trans' trans). For the first year of the course, I had a hard time of it. They were very Freudian, and their whole approach to LGBT people is that you 'become' LGBT as result of issues when you are young. As you can imagine, I had major difficulties with that. Since completing my initial training, I have become much more relational in my approach with gender diverse clients. A peer on the diploma course was outed for being gay as the course tutor.

"I did the Pink Therapy Gender Sexuality and Relationship Diversity essentials course. I have worked in the LGBT community in various guises for 25 years. Whilst training I worked part-time in HIV care, prevention, and sexual health. Today I only work in private practice.

"Five years ago, I came out as non-binary. I had noticed a shift, almost overnight, in my clients; from mostly gay men to a significant increase in the number of trans people. In my own therapy, I felt very connected. Then came an epiphany in understanding myself as non-binary; and now I only work with gender diverse clients.

"This has been a much harder journey for my parents than it ever was around being gay or queerness. So 'non-binary' is not part of any language my parents understand as there is a generational gap with this language. My mother told how me she had gone to a friend for Shabbat lunch and someone had been very transphobic. Mum got very defensive. I said that – getting defensive – was very unlike her. Was she telling me this, because it was part of my story? She said no. OK, I said: but I may as well tell you I am non-binary.

"She asked me not to do anything around transition, in her mind non-binary still meant transgender and her fear was me doing full medical transition. That is not what I was wanting."

"All the same, I do have some dysphoria, and I am looking for a slightly different shape. More androgynous, but not full feminisation. So, I will only do hormones up to a certain point, and when I start developing breast tissue, I will stop."

"The whole process has been drawn out by my GP deciding to gatekeep. I wanted a referral to fertility services before starting gender hormones. My GP started with 'you've lived as who you are for so long. Why do it now?'

"Then more delay, because before starting any sort of transition, I wanted to ensure that I preserved some fertility post HRT. I wanted my sperm frozen. Their take: 'It's not a priority. Because you have HIV and what about longevity of life.' They did not know that there is a special HIV route for fertility treatment. They should have known.

"It was galling because all the objections felt like ignorance. Worse, because NHS guidelines around hormones are so rooted in safeguarding, it sets up a fear on the part of the GP that they will be responsible for a major change. Eventually, my GP said I could go private for 16 weeks. I asked: 'What if I can't afford to?' Then one of my clients told me about a brilliant GP, and I moved to them.

"I am interested in where these barriers come from. Because I am also an activist. There is fear on both sides. Fear of safeguarding. Fear of what a patient will do next. The normal reaction would be to be more human. Instead, they just built a wall. They invited me in for an appointment. At the time I saw them, my dysphoria was bad. So, it struck me as odd that they were prepared to hand out very large doses of antidepressants with little in the way of additional checks. But they do not want to deal with the dysphoria.

"I questioned clinical opinion. They did not like that. After six years, I finally had an appointment with the NHS. I was shocked at how fast they were able to work. I was referred to TransPlus clinic on Dean St. They were happy to prescribe hormones.

"So, now I am getting a gender services referral. At the same time, I am moving forward on a path to fertility referral, with a private clinic. They are also putting together a bespoke route that takes hormones into account. I have just started gender hormones at about the same time as I finally got a fertility referral from the NHS. For now, I am taking an extreme low-dose to see if it prevents dysphoric feelings as I don't want full feminisation.

"It has been a long slow trek, and I am fascinated to see who is OK with my journey, who is not. I have been fortunate, as an adult, to find and join a very open-minded Jewish community. This is the Massorti Jewish community. It sits one level below Orthodox, and before Reform and Liberal.

"Beyond transition, I am still out there in the queer world; still attracted to men. Recently, though, I have been having sex with trans men and trans women. I am ready, through my own therapy work, to deal with shifts in desire. Even losing it altogether. But I have been shocked that some gay friends have had a real issue with my coming out as non-binary.

"Professionally, I have major issues with therapists who are there to gatekeep. Much too much fear, on both sides of the couch. Institutions are just starting to improve in their coverage of LGB issues in training. They are only now beginning to understand that training also needs to include gender diversity. The problem is that the national press sets up a fear of going into this area for everybody and this reinforces barriers.

"Separate from this is the fact that some strands of therapy are very pathologizing and medical. They come from the perspective that something needs to be fixed. But not in a positive way.

"I am absolutely not about pathologising trans or non-binary people. However, my LGBT services background makes me much more trans affirmative. A lot of clients arrive expecting me to be a gatekeeper. Whereas my approach is to see how someone can move forward and can build resilience and coping mechanisms while they are waiting.

"Working in HIV and sexual health, I am much more used to working in a holistic way. Looking at what needs they have; referring them to where these needs can be dealt with. That carries over to trans clients. So, if, for example, an individual is isolated, some of the therapy homework might be 'go to a trans support group.' See what it is like to be part of a community.

"I also do supervision for other therapists. It is fascinating to be on that side of the street. It is also a good time to challenge them. I ask if they should be working in this area if they have not had specific gender diverse training. Because they are not separating their issues from what the client is bringing. Personally, I believe that therapists training through seeing clients is not ethical.

"It has been a long and difficult road. I've not arrived yet, but I am getting there. Following being on the interfaith panel at Pink Therapy's *Intersectional Conference,* my paper *'The Chicken Soup of Identity'* was accepted for a book called *'Non-Binary Lives: An Anthology of Intersecting Identities'* (editor Dr Jos Twist, Tavistock and Portman NHS Trust; associate editors: Dr Meg-Jon Barker, Dr Ben Vincent and Dr Kat Gupta; published by Jessica Kingsley Publishers). *'Non-Binary Lives'* made number one LGBTQ+ book in The Independent's Best Book Buys of 2020[40], and Best Reads for Pride 2020. Do get it. It's well worth a read."

Chrissie: not denying any more

Like many trans women, Chrissie knew from an early age, before she even started primary school, that she was different. She tells me: "I knew I was queer/trans since I was four or five. But I was shamed by my father as a young child, for my feminine

40 Waite-Taylor, E. (2020). IndyBest's Best Book Buys for 2020: From 'How to Fail' to 'Light Years.' *The Independent.* [online] 31 Dec. Available at: https://www.independent.co.uk/extras/indybest/books/best-indybest-books-2020-uk-b1776981.html.

being and dressing in feminine clothes. So, I buried my true self. I hid who I was from the world. So deeply that I lost touch with my own soul.

"Undiagnosed gender dysphoria and dysmorphia meant I was totally dysfunctional, if not absent, even when in school. I ran away from home when I was 16. I became a drug dealer and teetered on the brink of prostitution. I was totally dependent upon alcohol and drugs to survive. To escape this hell, I ran away, to India, where I succumbed to opium addiction. I ended up begging on the streets of Old Delhi and experienced a total breakdown. I was just twenty-one. All this self-abuse had been an unconscious seeking to obliterate the pain of who I really was.

"In this broken and derelict state, I encountered the love of Christ. Rescued and repatriated by aid workers, back home, I went cold turkey. I suffered a total psychotic breakdown. The vicar of a local church answered my mother's distressed call for help.

"He and another vicar put me through an exorcism. To this day, I do not know what happened in that exorcism, or whether it had any effect at all.

"My desire to follow Christ led me to fall into this church. The vicar again shamed me for being feminine in my soul. He put me through deliverance ministry as conversion therapy. This middle class, middle of the road church saw my 'conversion' to their faith as a major victory. Every time there was an evangelistic event, I was asked to speak, to tell my story. People would start to gently cry, as they experienced the love that had transformed my life. People told me I should write my story into a book. Yet every time I told it, I was burying the truth about my struggles with my gender and sexuality in even deeper denial. I too had been 'brainwashed' to believe they were 'sinful.'

"For thirty years or more I tried to be the successful Christian. I wore the mask of toxic masculinity and spirituality. A performative Christianity, a 'fig leaf' to cover my deep sense of shame. Husband, father, missionary, Pastor. Two beautiful daughters. I had been assistant pastor in a conservative church whose pastor believed he could heal gay people. I preached grace. Yet it had still not touched the deepest part of who I was.

"The first crack – though I did not know it then – appeared in 2007. I started my own business. I bought a laptop, and at that point I started to write my story. It took me about three years. I left it sat on my computer, gathering dust, knowing there was a vital missing chapter, that the story was not finished, but I had no idea what that missing chapter was.

"I had been in total denial about my transness for almost five decades. External pressures were crushing me: the recession, my building business almost running at a loss. We lost our parents in painful deaths. Our daughter suffered life-threatening illness, both my wife and I were battling depression. I discovered deep down in myself, not faith in a loving God, but an even deeper shame about who I really was. The foundations of my personal faith were shame.

"2014 was seen by many as the year the 'transgender

phenomenon' broke in western consciousness. Laverne Cox was on the front cover of Time magazine, under the headline, 'Transgender Tipping Point, are trans rights the new human rights frontier?'

"In the US Caitlyn Jenner was headline news. In the UK Frank Mallone became Kelly Malone. The word transgender was trending everywhere. Transgender was the viral news shock.

"I honestly did not even know, then, what the word meant. I had hidden from all those conversations in the 'holy bubble' of church. Yet, instinctively, I knew that I was transgender, and had been all my conscious life. Shame and fear paralysed me, my faith evaporated and I found myself in a permanent suicidal state. I had battled a subconscious self-hatred and suicidal ideation all my life. Now it crushed me.

"I began dressing, trying to find myself. But the self-hatred only increased. I began drinking heavily. I would climb in the car, blind drunk, and drive down the motorway at high speed. I was hoping to kill myself in an 'accident.'

"In this state, I suddenly realised I might not kill myself, but someone else's partner, child, or parent. I sobered in an instant, with the realisation that the only sane thing to do was walk into the light, and be honest about who I really am. I was terrified of telling anyone.

"I came out to myself as trans. I was 54.

"I knew, instantly, that this was the missing the chapter of my book. But far bigger than that, my book had been a work of fiction. A fabrication. A total denial of my true self and my lost soul.

"Six months later, I knew I had to tell my wife. Away from home on work, I wrote her a love letter, together with an explanation of who I really was. I wrote non-stop for almost twenty-four hours. Arriving home, I thought I was about to lose everything, my wife, my family, my home, my career, my community. I gave her the letter. We held hands, and read it together. We both wept. She was shocked and devastated. Yet it was at this point that our faith really played its part.

"We were both very damaged; both children from seriously broken backgrounds, parents with multiple divorces. We knew, from the start, that the only way that our marriage would work was if we first, as individuals, committed to following Christ. This was the basis for our marriage: love Christ before one another. That may seem strange to those of other faiths. Yet it was what saved us now.

"She committed to love me, no matter what life might throw at us.

"I will not deny it has been very difficult. For both of us. My wife had a very conservative evangelical faith. The issue I faced – we faced - was how to balance the needs of a family with my crushing gender dysphoria and dysmorphia.

"I came out to my closest Christian friends in 2016. They turned their backs on me.

"In coming out, I had expected to experience the judgement, anger, and wrath of God. Instead, what I discovered was the overwhelming, outrageous, love of God. My shame and life-long suicidal ideation simply evaporated. It was the judgement and rejection of conservative evangelicals that stunned me.

"I went to Oxford's John Radcliffe Hospital for psychiatric evaluation in 2017, in the hope of eventually transitioning. The psychiatrist told me I could access hormones, laser treatment, and surgery. I replied that I did not wish to risk losing my family by transitioning immediately. But I needed counselling to help with the traumas we had been through. He told me there was nothing available.

"That put me to the back of the queue, and at 65, I now have no hope of being seen, or treated by the NHS for my crippling gender dysphoria and dysmorphia.

"2019, I came out publicly as transfemme. I transitioned to live my life as Chrissie. I also finally had a hip replacement, after years of living in chronic pain. Before recovering from my hip surgery, Covid laid me out on my bed for several months. I had promised myself that I would use the bed rest from surgery to re-write my story. Now, as I endured almost a year of being bed-ridden, was the obvious time to complete the story.

"Tina Beardsley (I call her mum), a trans woman and priest in the Church of England, suggested her own publishers to me. I had no hope of finding a publisher. Still, I thought I should at least try, or regret it forever. DLT Publishers loved my writing. I had found a publisher with my first submission?!?! A dream come true.

"The book[41] was published July 2021.

41 Chevasutt, C. (2021). *Heaven Come Down: The story of a transgender disciple.*

"Three months later, friends pointed me to a job advert, for an outreach worker to the trans community, for a church, in my home city. I didn't bother applying. I knew it would go to an ordained minister, with a Masters in Divinity, and decades of pastoral ministry.

"The weekend applications closed, a trans friend called from London. Had I applied for the job? It had my name all over it! My wife and two daughters thought I was crazy not applying. I frantically cobbled together a pathetic CV over the weekend.

"January 2022, I started work in my dream job, 'Outreach and Development Worker with Transgender, Intersex, and Non-binary People' for Saint Columba's United Reformed Church.

"We designated the first year as a research year, to network and build relationships of trust. Listening to the community, and establishing needs. From this we might be able to see and understand what the role might be able to do with the transgender community.

"In the first three months of 2022, there were three young trans suicides. A fifteen-year-old trans girl, in the village next to mine, never came home after experiencing online harassment at school. A fifteen-year-old trans boy took his own life, in Bicester, just a few miles away. He was known and loved within the Oxford trans community. A transman, in his early twenties, working for a large trans charity, known by my neighbour, ordered chemicals online and took his own life. His Christian

---

London: Dartman Longford Todd Publishers.

fundamentalist parents could not accept him for who he was.

"My role and ministry are all about trying to help save vulnerable young trans lives. To do this, we needed maximum visibility. To show young trans people there is help, pastoral and medical, always available to them.

"We think there are about 1,000 trans, non-binary, and intersex students in Oxford, between the two universities. I am engaged in pastoral ministry within the student trans and LGBT+ community. This pastoral ministry shapes and informs a lot of what I do. Through heart-breaking conversations with trans students, we realised many LGBT+ students are wounded. Spiritually abused by conservative evangelical churches and clergy.

"The Oxford Diocese, and other denominations, seem to be denying the very painful reality experienced by LGBT+ students. This has brought me into direct conflict with the religious powers that rule from on high.

"I'm in the final year of my contract. My work has become focussed on the trauma experienced by students and young people, and issues of safeguarding, restorative justice, restitution, and the healing of victims and survivors of church or spiritual abuse.

"Sometimes, the trauma and pain are too much. Over Christmas, I found myself empty, drained, spent. Totally depressed. I spent a few days just staring at the walls. Christmas day, I broke down and wept in front of my family.

"I pick myself up, and carry on. Ultimately, I find meaning

and purpose through loving and serving the trans community. It helps dissipate the intensity of my own perpetual gender dysphoria and dysmorphia. I feel I have done something of worth with my life. If God is love, then I've given them, and my community, my best."

Shea: Out and Pride

Shea is 50x: a trans woman who has been out for 5 years. Not only this, but she is in a relationship with a partner of 18 years. And they live together in a house in Medway – from which she directs both Medway Pride and Medway Radio. Busy bee!

For that reason, the following is not quite interview, as others have been. Rather, it is a piece of personal writing, submitted by Shea specifically for this book.

She writes:

The one thing you never want when you go and see your GP is to have them laugh in your face!

My first experience of coming out to someone not in my immediate family was to my GP. Six weeks after telling my family I summoned up the courage to make an appointment, and ask my GP to refer me to the Gender Identity Clinic in London.

I turned up alone to the appointment. That was a mistake I have made sure I never made again. The usual lengthy delay. Finally, they called me in. Coming out can be freeing. It makes you feel lighter, and able to start being you. Before that, though, at the point you speak up, you are vulnerable.

I stumbled through my planned speech, as nervous as I have ever been. I could not make eye contact; just wanted to get through this, speak up, get referred. I mean, it will be OK right? GP's have to deal with all sorts of heath care issues.

I wasn't prepared for the appointment. I know that now. If you are dealing with the NHS for any kind of gender care, be prepared. Be spectacularly prepared. Go armed with facts, figures, clippings, notes: anything that you may need. Follow that up with another file full of anything you think you won't need. What I didn't know at the time is that many GPs, nurses, and other NHS staff simply do not have enough knowledge about gender issues. Neither do they care to find out.

I certainly wasn't prepared for the silence that followed. The GP's face said it all. My innermost fears; my worries about coming out; all encapsulated on a face barely suppressing a laugh.

"I'm just going to consult a colleague." She stood up and left the room. I could not help but feel she had gone outside for a laugh at my expense. Long minutes passed, and I thought about just leaving. I felt deflated, scared, and sure that the whole practice was now in on the joke. Only the fear of having to walk through reception, with all the staff nudging and pointing, kept me rooted to the chair.

The door opened. The GP came back in, and it was obvious she had been laughing. She sat back at the laptop, and now it was her turn not to make eye contact. For fear of laughing again? She mumbled something about a form and attempted to find it digitally. A couple of minutes later she was back out consulting a colleague. Then back in, form found. She looked it over.

"This is a very long form." She stared at it like a mountaineer studying the North Face of the Eiger. Then she made a snap decision.

"I think it would be best if you went home and had a good think about this."

She reached for a post-it note, wrote something on it and handed it to me. 'Have a good think' were her final words. On the note were details of the website for the GIC. It was a web address that I, like many trans people, knew by heart. It tells you to see your GP for a referral.

I left in a state of shock that I had received such treatment. It took 9 months, 3 complaints, a new practice manager and a recorded telephone consultation before I was able to get a referral.

That was over 3 years ago. I am still waiting for my first appointment.

After a long wait, and much fighting, I found myself in the fortunate position where I could access surgeries privately. After the experience with my local GP, I self-referred to a private health care service. There I was quickly and safely able to get advice, guidance, tests, and eventually hormones. Unfortunately, this provider does not do surgeries. As I said, you need to know all about the subject if you want to find your way around the gender care maze.

I phoned my local private healthcare hospital which is based in Medway. I explained I was trans, and looking for breast augmentation. I told them I could fund it privately. The lady was delightful and I booked an initial consultation.

10 days later my wife and I turned up to the private hospital. We were shown in right on time. The consultant was a woman, but presented quite masculine. I know we should not judge, but in this case, it made me feel more comfortable.

We sat down, the lady turned to my wife and said, "How can I help you?"

My heart sank, I explained that the appointment was for me. I told her that I was a Trans woman. I was now seeking breast augmentation after having been on hormones for 3 years.

'I think you have to be on hormones for 5 years before any form of surgery,' she replied. This is absolutely why you have to have a witness to what is said!

She grudgingly took my details, filled out forms, and told me there was a 2-week cooling off period. Somewhere I heard a door slam. I was then told to bring a bra of the size I wished to be to the next appointment. In the car on the way home my wife remained chipper. But I'd been fighting so long I did not want to get any hopes up.

Two weeks later we went back with the bra, and I 'tried on' breasts. This is a surreal experience. But it did bring me joy, seeing how I might look after surgery. We agreed that the size I wanted was correct for my frame. Photos were taken. I felt that we were progressing.

Once I was fully clothed again the consultant said they had some questions they needed clarity on from the clinic. She would be in touch within 10-14 days to confirm the next step.

Guess what? That was four months ago. Despite repeated emails to the consultant's secretary, they are still waiting. For clarity around questions they won't tell me about.

Of course, those 2 appointments cost several hundred pounds. She was more than happy to take payment for those.

I am now on the waiting list for another clinic. It's a four month wait for a possible first appointment. The word 'possible' is the operative word in that sentence.

I still carry that post-it note from the GP with me. I show it at talks I do. A while back, a family member asked me when I decided to become a "Campaigner." Oh, the emphasis of disgust on the word! Campaigner...

The answer is when I got the post-it note. But should anyone still have to fight for healthcare?

Rhiannon: afraid again

At 53, Rhiannon is now living her good life. Sort of. She finally got to transition a few years back. That makes her happy. Sadly, though, she is also witness and victim of 'cis enforcement' at its finest. To wit: away with those nasty queer vibes! Or we'll beat them out of you.

Her first inkling of transness was in the playground in primary school. She tells me: "I was playing with friends: all girls. A teacher came up. They told me: 'leave the girls alone and go play with the boys.' That was the first time I knew something was different. I was maybe 6 at the time.

"The boys bullied me because I hung around with girls. So, I tried to fit in. I did stuff like sports I mostly didn't like. Doing 'manly things.' Because if I didn't, my dad would say 'Don't be a sissy.' I never did fit into parental expectations of their 'little boy.' They always described me as 'sensitive.'

"Secondary school was a nightmare. A new bunch of kids, and I stuck out like a sore thumb. There was one boy that I hung out with in primary. But when we got to secondary school, he started to bully me, too. One day he poured perfume all over me. I was terrified that 'they knew.' So, when we got off the bus on the way home, I beat him up. Not my finest moment; but it stopped (some of) the bullying.

"Years later, I met him again. He had come out as gay man. He told me that he was starting to get bullied, himself. So, he deflected onto another kid, hoping others would not spot him. In secondary school, I did not have the language to explain my feelings. But I was starting to see trans folks on the TV. Though mostly this was Sunday news headlines, and they were never positive. I felt I could never tell anyone.

"I joined the army cadets. I played rugby. I tried to fit every stereotype. That was when depression and anxiety first hit. In secondary school. I just didn't want to be there anymore. I guess that impacted my university too. I started. Then I quit. I loved music; was studying music, and wanted to be in the music business. A rock star! My parents weren't altogether happy with that. Still, I went off and played in bands for years.

"That became a sort of mask. Because the 80s were the era of 'hair metal'. That's a lighter version of heavy metal, dominated by men who were very effeminate. Even though they sang some quite misogynist songs. It was a place I could be without being exactly out.

"I came out to some close friends. I was sharing a house in the mid-90s with two women: one lesbian, one bi. One day we were watching Paddington Green on TV. It was ground-breaking at the time, because one of the characters, Jackie McAuliffe, was a trans woman. My house-mates were saying positive things about Jackie. As the credits rolled, I turned to the two of them, and said: 'I'm just like her.' They said 'that makes sense.'

"They were very supportive. One offered to help me with make-up, dressing, and so on. Thus began my first attempt at transition. But I was working at the time in a service industry - electronic repair – which was wholly male. At work I was 'this guy.' Then, I'd come home and be me. It was a weird split existence. I started coming out to more and more people, including my parents.

"Then, around New Year's Eve, towards the end of the 90's. there was a big party in the house. The boyfriend of one of my friends followed me into the bathroom, and beat me up. Next day I left the house and never went back.

"In my 30s, and living with parents again! Within a couple of months, I'd got rid of pretty much everything to do with who I was. Back in the closet. 'Detransitioned' – but not because I wasn't trans. I did not come out again, properly, for 12 years. I just felt there was no place for me in that world. A week or two after the party, I started cutting. I even tried to take my life.

"A bit later, I moved out and started to dip my toe in the water again. But it was furtive stuff. Just occasional dressing at night as a way of proving I was still there. In 2002, I met someone who was positive. At least, when I told her about me, she said 'OK. I can live with that for a bit and see how it goes.' At least, she was fine with me expressing myself as femme in the house. But she said she was afraid if I went out as me, we might get a brick through the window. I started to come out to more people again.

"We lasted 12 years. In 2012, I decided no longer wanted to do a job where I could not be me. Now, my partner was OK with this, and was amazed that colleagues were 90% supportive. At about the same time, I quit a band I was in, because a lot of the band members were very homophobic.

"We stayed together another 2 years. Then it fell apart, as the reality of medical transition loomed. I remember it well. 30 August 2014. Because that was the same day I went to the historic meeting between the trans community and Stonewall. At the time, I was starting to get involved in the politics of it. I was also being a bit selfish, which I think I had to be to get through transition.

"She said: 'I can't do this anymore.' I had to move house; ended up sofa surfing, because I could not find anywhere to live. Briefly it got acrimonious. Since then, though, we have had a good friendship. Mostly.

"But here I was in 2014. No job. No money. No proper address. This is where I started my medical transition, in February in a freezing cold caravan, having sweats and hot flushes. If friends had not been prepared to loan their caravan, I would have been homeless.

"I wish I could say good things about the NHS. Mostly, though, they were awful. I tried to transition in the 90's, but got nowhere. I was referred to a psychosocial counsellor, who diagnosed 'anxiety and depression.'

"In 2012, I spoke to my GP, who told me it could be 2 to 3 years before I got to see anyone in the Wales area. 2 months later, they had retired, and I had a new GP, who was much more pro-active. They contacted Charing Cross, and referred me to local mental health services. That took 2 to 3 months. Then he referred me onto Welsh specialised services who were meant to greenlight spending. After 8 months we'd heard nothing and no referral had been received. So, we asked the Welsh service if they could send a copy of the letter to Charing Cross. They refused.

"I went back to my GP and got him to print off a copy of the Welsh services letter. Luckily, he still had it on file. It was never clear what had happened, but it looks like the Welsh service had raised a letter, but never sent it. Incompetence? Transphobia? A bit of both, likely.

"Charing Cross were fantastic; though it took three appointments before they said yes to hormones. There were also lengthy gaps between each appointment; and a different clinician every time. It took me three years from first visit to my discharge in 2018, following gender confirmation surgery.

"Even then, the cock-ups continued. The surgical referral was sent to the wrong surgeon. They could not do the surgery, because of internal NHS charging rules. That meant I had to get my final sign-off again, because the signature had 'expired.'

"It was a constant impact on my mental health. Up, down; up, down. But by then, my life was much more stable. Back in 2012, I started volunteering with charities. They asked me to do more and more. I met new people. My circle of contacts was growing, and I started bringing in work for myself. Now I'm working for a trans-supportive charity. I've finally found a career where being trans is no longer an issue!

"For the most part, life is great. Family is very supportive. Dad sadly passed. But not a single negative reaction. I was afraid they would react badly. I guess they got over it when I told them first time round. I have a great job. Great friends.

"I've never been happier. The treatment fixed what it needed to fix and fixed it incredibly well. Before I started to transition, I felt jealous of every woman I saw walking down the street. That's completely gone away.

"The one fly in the ointment now is safety. I never doubted who I am. My 'detransition' was never about doubt, so much as fear. Then, for a while, that went away. But since all the nastiness in politics and the media over the last few years, starting to worry about safety in public.

"I am afraid again."

Theodore: young, wise

Some stories, some conversations, are truly delightful. So it was when finally I got to speak to Theodore. At 18, they are the youngest of our interviewees. Still mid-exams; looking forward to going to university to study medicine.

They tell me: "I identify as transgender - transmasc – and am still trying to figure out if I identify as non-binary. It works, but I'm not sure I like that label for me. I am also autistic, and I live in Scotland.

"I usually say that my pronouns are 'he/him.' With people who are more accepting, 'he/they/it.' I don't expect people to use neopronouns so when they do it feels like an extra 'treat.'

"I guess the first signs were in the playground. I found myself always playing with boys. I identified with masc characters. Maybe I would've identified with non-binary characters but there wasn't really any representation of that. "Somewhere between 9 and 13 I started to understand this as a difference. I decided to come out to a friend. But as luck would have it, they came out to me first! So, I said: 'Don't worry; I'm trans too. Then I started telling my other friends.

"I was worried about my parents. They are important to me despite an upbringing where their actions led me to go into therapy for trauma work for emotional and verbal abuse. I don't think this was due to malicious intent on their part. They are good people who have done bad things, and it's difficult to reconcile with this. But people are complicated and understanding doesn't mean forgiveness.

"Coming out was emotional. I started with my dad because I felt he would be more receptive. He was understanding at first. He said he was glad I could tell him. He said he still loved me. Then he started questioning. I asked him not to tell mum, as she had made homophobic comments previously. He agreed. But then he went ahead and told mum anyway. Even though I can kind of understand, that was a major betrayal of trust.

"Next day they presented a united front. 'We don't believe you are trans. You're too young to know. Did we raise you wrong? Maybe you're a tomboy.' And so on. So, I went back into the closet for two more years. I was very upset. But I was also grappling with other stuff at the time.

"But my sense of identity did not change. So, I picked up again when I was 14/15-ish. I was still using he/him pronouns online which may have been another sign. I got a binder and that caused a lot of upset within the family. Mum figured it out and Dad told me 'No LGBT in the house.' Their attitude was 'Once you turn 18, we cannot stop you. We won't disown you. We just won't approve and we are afraid for your future/safety.'

"I just wish they could be more open. But their opposition

is from their upbringing in China, and it's difficult to change opinions you have been brought up with. In China, the general attitude is that trans is rare. Also, it is hard to transition, and if you do, then you must transition in a binary way. It is ironic that a lot of LGBT things have been shut down lately since one of the most iconic personalities – Jin Xing - is openly trans.

"I think the community-focused culture has been used to perpetuate bigotry. In some ways, I prefer the collective culture to western individualism. But it can also foster a view of outsiders as 'other.' Therefore, no longer part of the community and 'wrong.' I hope in the future we can acknowledge and support individuality but still have strong communities.

"I haven't engaged with the medical system a lot when it comes to transitioning. I spoke to my GP when I was14. They said if one day I wanted to transition, they could help. They introduced me to Glasgow GIC. But the system prefers self-referral, and I cannot do that because of the inevitable emotional fall-out at home.

"Still, I get to express myself as I am now 18." (T has wonderful rainbow hair. I am jealous!)

"My dad didn't speak to me for days after my first short haircut, but he didn't speak about dyed hair so I am as hopeful as I can allow myself to be.

"It is important to understand that my first coming out isn't what matters most to me despite its importance, but the subsequent ones and what happened after. I don't make much effort to be perceived in a stereotypical masculine sense, as thankfully I do not experience dysphoria which limits my (gender) expression too much. After I'm further in my own transition journey, I would like to wear dresses. So, I came out to everyone to not be misgendered.

"Teachers like me, because I get good grades and perform well. But only one teacher has respected my name and pronouns, without school telling them to. I think part of the issue was their misunderstanding of Scottish guidance around informal name change. None of them would use my name and pronouns even in private. So, they would say 'I support you' and 'I believe who you are.' But they feel they are not allowed to be open about it.

"One teacher said 'You can tell the class.' I really respect that she found it within herself to do that. Otherwise, teachers misgendered and deadnamed me despite knowing. At 16, I just changed my name across the board. Because if my parents can't do anything, they won't. Since then, I've been talking to school management about their policies. I've done two teacher training days with new management, as they need to hear about this stuff.

"There's a long way to go, especially when it comes to understanding intersectionality and queerness outside the binary. There is also the issue that this is not mandatory training for teachers. It's elective. This needs to change. There are still too many members of staff who don't get it and cause harm with or without meaning to. Meanwhile, 'management' are the HR department for most schools. They're almost never on your side.

"I know I won't change minds overnight. At least, if they have contact with people who can talk to them, persuade them, there is some chance we might humanise the LGBT people a little.

"I came out to some of my Chinese relatives. One lives in the UK, and that was easy. She was open-minded, and could relate to what I told her with having some different values than your family. I came out to a cousin in China. Her response: 'Different people are why the world is interesting' The younger generations are much more accepting and of course no group is a monolith.

"On the other hand, she advised me not to come out to my grandfather. He is generally supportive, and makes allowances for my 'difference.' My hair. Dating a non-Chinese. But she felt this was a difference too far.

"I experience social dysphoria because the world genders things. I am afraid of being 'misunderstood.' So, I'm happy just to let sleeping dogs lie since he doesn't view gender as a big thing. He is not unaware. And sometimes you don't have to say.

"I have recently had opportunities to know more older queer people personally. It's wonderful. Because basically all of my life, the oldest queer I have known has been... me. So, I've always felt a responsibility to help others. Now that I'm out in the world, it's cool to be meeting people. Great to be able to be young and learn again."

Afterword

If you've got this far, you'll know a good deal more about what it means to be trans in the UK today. Who we are. Some law. Some history. Above all, you'll have read some (very) personal experiences.

They are eye-opening, in all sorts of ways. For starters, there really is no single trans narrative. No standard. That might come as a bit of a shock to the eminent von Krafft-Ebing, who pretty much single-handedly defined 'transness.' In much the same way as a naturalist might describe (and prescribe) the normal mating behaviour of walruses. With about as much science as Freud brought to the discovery of the Oedipus Complex. And rather less than is required nowadays if trans people are to receive medical treatment in the UK.

Many realised that something was up at 4/5. Others not until puberty. Yet others came to it late. I am a good example of that. I knew something was wrong pretty much throughout my life. Yet, I never really understood 'trans' as anything much more than vicars wearing dresses on a Sunday afternoon. Figures of fun.

Even now, that is not uncommon. Some of those I spoke to said they had no idea what trans was until they were in their 20's. Or later. Though many of those reported 'something up' long before then.

Factors influencing when and how people came out include

general awareness. The more you tell people about transness, the more open trans people there will be. Because awareness does not make people *more* trans; it makes them *less* fearful. But also, and quite significant, given recent attempts by government to make outing trans school kids compulsory, is fear of parental reaction. Sometimes that may turn out to be ill-founded. Sometimes, it is real, with several talking of threats of violence. From parents. Also, parents disowning them or doing all they could to slow transition down.

For that reason, many waited years to tell their parents. Or they waited until they could not wait any longer or were about to leave home. So much for alleged 'rapid onset gender dysphoria': another anti-trans piece of science, soundly debunked. Perhaps someone should carry out research into when trans people told parents, and how long after they knew they were trans before they did so.

Meanwhile, take no notice of sensationalist media narratives about schools 'transing kids.' The consensus from several interviewees was that sex ed was about as useful as a chocolate teapot. Trans was not really covered, or just barely got a mention. 'There are gay people. There are also trans people. The end.'

Here was going to be a long and heartfelt diatribe on the iniquities of the UK press. Its obsession with trans people, leading to a more than 100-fold increase in pieces about 'trans issues' in the decade 2012-2022. The vast majority, hostile.

The disinformation. The trashing of basic journalistic standards by the *Times, Telegraph, Mail, Guardian*. The imbalance. Because while libel law makes writing about any individual – particularly any wealthy individual – fraught with danger, there is no such counter-balance to a press that liberally sprinkles its pieces with untruths about minorities. Not just the inevitable 'trans rights activists' – but any group that dares raise its voice in defense of its own.

It is almost 35 years since Home Office minister David Mellor declared that the UK media were "drinking in last chance saloon". Yet this still feels like unfinished business.

So, let us pass by, taking a moment merely to reflect on one story you won't have seen this week. For as credible reports emerge, from whistle blowers, that the NHS pivot to anti-trans policies may have contributed to the deaths of 16 young trans people, the last 24 hours of news – with a few honourable exceptions from braver journalists - has been focussed wholly on... how Keir Starmer has met one very wealthy author, whose public commentary on trans people regularly gives rise to outrage within that community. That, though, is an entirely other book.

Of course, it needs investigating. 'Standing up.' Yet seeing the vast acres of print devoted to the least anti-trans rumour, this indifference does not feel accidental.

While parental violence was not marked, parental interference was significant. Many folks had to leave home. That made them technically homeless. That, in turn, made it much harder to transition. It also makes young trans people that much more vulnerable.

In terms of parental delay, loads of tactics were used, including every which way of gaming the psych system. 'You can transition, but only after you have been assessed for autism' was a line spun to more than one individual.

Then, there were loads of delays, from a system that feels unfit for purpose. I spoke to a few non-UK trans people. Compared to the UK, they positively whizzed through the system. Next to many other countries, UK gender care is simply broken. More than one instance of individuals being done and dusted for surgery in the time it took the UK system not to get back to them with a first appointment.

Once inside the system there were a few positive reviews. Mostly, it felt, from older trans women who, I'm guessing, put up with less nonsense. Young trans guys, though, had some horror stories. Being told how long their hair should be. Asked to 'define a man.' Not being listened to. Threatened. In at least one instance, there was an explicit threat that if the individual continued to displease, they would be barred from transition.

GP's again a mixed bag. There are multiple stories of GP's sticking an oar in... refusing to allow bridging prescriptions, refusing even to honour shared care agreements. Beyond the stories here, we know this is getting worse. Because faced with a broken system, trans people are resorting to workarounds, en masse. These, in turn, have been classed as 'loopholes' by government and establishment alike. As though transitioning is some sort of crime. Government seeks to plug loopholes. GP's become more trans-sceptic. So trans folk resort to more and more dangerous alternatives. What else would you expect?

Is this 'conversion therapy'? I suspect many would claim it is just standard medical caution. Except, when psychs can keep you in limbo for 4, 5, 6 years for an issue that is not a mental health matter, it absolutely smells like conversion therapy to me. As for caution, this is anything but 'standard.' Again, as both the stories and accompanying background make clear, there appears to be one standard applied to trans people; one standard for everyone else. I will, perhaps, believe trans people are subject to the same rules as everyone else when cis folks are required to undergo psych counselling before they get married, or have a child. For these are both significant life-changing events.

Too, the UK system contrasts dramatically with other systems where psychs' role is to support. Their job is to help to identify roadblocks. To discuss issues. Because they do not act as gatekeepers, they exert a much more positive influence on the process.

In this respect, a story that made me truly sick was that of the young trans woman, aged 26, who had spent years trying to persuade UK psychs to allow her some HRT. She already had clear and obvious hair loss. For many trans women that is one of the worst possible things. Yet despite some 5 years talking to the gender service, not one psych, at any point, mentioned or identified hair loss as any sort of issue.

One might think that a psych who (claimed to) understand trans people and trans healthcare would have noticed. Might, at least, have prescribed a testosterone blocker just to allow some time. But no. Nothing.

Beyond that? Most folks seem to have transitioned with little incident at work. But not entirely without incident. Perhaps more significant, still, is the influence that religion still has on acceptance. More than a few instances of 'Christians' disowning trans relatives. Though when it comes to bigotry, other religions are available, too.

Beyond that, the simple questions that cis people in the UK today need to answer are: do you believe trans people are who they say they are? And do we deserve rights?

In respect of the first, we have been defined by a non-scientist. Since then, there has been a queue, a mile long, of "experts" lining up to explain us away. There are "a few true transsexuals" but now it's all just "autistic transtrenders who must be protected from peer pressure." Or "perverts and fetishists." Or, just people who are mentally ill!

These are simplistic takes. Reductive in the extreme. They fail to consider the possibility that transness represents a complex interplay between biology and sociology. Or to notice that other countries have a far more nuanced take on all this than in we have had in the UK of late. Perhaps, ever.

Alongside sits all of the prejudice. Being trans "is a less desirable outcome than not being trans." Because trans people are "a threat." Because they are "ick." So, all that can be done to stop people transitioning is "fair game."

Whereas, the moment one begins to accept that trans

people are real; that we are who we say we are; most of this falls away. In particular, our response to trans kids. If transness is something one knows from an early age, then enforcing a cis puberty on a trans kid is not being helpful. Or nice. Or merciful. It is abuse of the cruellest type.

There is abundant evidence that we are real, and a real minority, in the same way that gay people or people from ethnic minorities are real. Evidence, too, that we will continue to exist no matter what is done to us. Against this, it becomes impossible to justify doing what is being done to us while maintaining any pretence at being 'one of the good people.'

But 'liberal democracies' have long had issues when faced with rights for people who confound the neat categories upon which their moral certitude rests.

In the end, this has nothing to do with an imagined culture war. The real question is: 'do trans people deserve rights?' Current evidence suggests that there is a disturbingly large number of people in positions of power in the UK whose answer to that question would be a resounding NO.

Resource

There is plenty of very good resource out there. As ever, a simple search online will turn up loads of links; and a bit of common sense will quickly weed out the outliers. Still, a good place to start is with the TransActual website. Here you will find simple explainers of many of the topics covered in this book, in-depth research reports, and onward links to more resources. This can be found, as of summer 2024, at www.transactual.org.uk.

This is useful for

- MPs: who to turn to if you need policy advice or how to help constituents who come with complex complaints about their healthcare;
- Medics: the site outlines training options and general directions in which you might do useful advocacy;
- Journos: because it helps to be at least a bit briefed on a subject before asking questions.
- Trans people: for when you face transphobia in your day-to-day life, and are looking for advice, resource, and help to fight back;
- Cis people: because the best way to educate yourself about trans people is to read what we have written on our own behalf.

Acknowledgments

In putting together this book, I am indebted to many individuals who have been seriously supportive throughout.

For the section on medical history, my thanks to Zoë Playdon. Zoë is the Emeritus Professor of Medical Humanities at the University of London, a Visiting Professor at the University of Cumbria, and an Honorary Research Fellow at Birkbeck College. Also, author of *The Hidden Case of Ewan Forbes.*

Her book sets out the bitter history of how trans people lost their human rights in the 1960s. Here, I have drawn heavily on an article that she wrote for TransActual UK. Also, we have spent time in conversation exploring the finer details of her narrative.

For editing and the strictest of proofreading, Jennie Kermode has been an invaluable help.

For the overall design of the book, and sourcing of poems, my thanks to Dorian Rose, who is also the founder of Transmuted. Thanks, obviously, due to the poets whose work is included here.

For commentary, feedback and correcting, to my fellow directors at TransActual.

Last, but absolutely not least, my thanks to every individual who came forward and took the time, the effort, to tell me their story. I know that for many that was not easy; was all too often an incredibly scary thing to do.

Thank you.